WALK
YOUR WAY
to better

Joyce Shulman

Kibo Press

Front cover design by Kamelija Gievska
Front cover photo by Lauren Kress

ISBN: 978-1-7342576-0-1

Library of Congress Control Number:2019920502

First printing edition 2019.

Kibo Press
99 Highview Drive
Sag Harbor, NY 11963

www.walkyourwaytobetter.com
www.joyceshulman.com

Table of Contents

Prologue

Here's What Happened

Everyone else in the house was sleeping. It was 2 a.m. and there I lay in my childhood bedroom, unchanged during the 18 months I'd been away at college.

I was sweating.

Sleep was impossible.

I shouldn't have eaten the chocolate cake, and I definitely shouldn't have eaten the second piece. I was angry with myself, and my stomach roiled in objection. But it was the holidays—you are supposed to indulge, right? It was the end of a three-week holiday break during my sophomore year of college. My hand rested on my belly.

Just after my 17th birthday, I'd left home as part of an early admission program that allowed me to enter college after my junior year of high school. Learning to live on my own, navigating the immense University of Maryland campus, balancing my freshman class load, plus two daily dance classes (I started as a dance major), and living with a roommate with whom I fought constantly, had been a whirlwind.

There were new friends, new boys, dormitory food, and late night pizza runs. There was the modern dance teacher who seemed to be a hundred years old and wore a faded green unitard every day, and the ballet teacher who made it very, very clear that I did *not* deserve a spot on her barre (she was right).

I climbed out of bed and dragged the old yellow scale out from under the bathroom sink. Gingerly, I stepped on, willing myself to be as light as possible.

It didn't work. In just 18 months, I had added close to 40 pounds to my 5-foot, 3-inch frame.

But, I thought, *how was that possible? I'm a dance major. How had I not even noticed the pounds piling on?*

I crawled back into my bed and cried. I cried because I couldn't believe I hadn't noticed how quickly I was gaining weight. I cried because I was scared that if I kept going this way, by the time I graduated, I'd have gained 100 pounds.

And I cried because my life felt out of control. I cried about the "D" I got in accounting because I thought I could blow off that hateful 8 a.m. class. I cried about the friends I missed from home. I cried about the hateful roommate.

I don't remember the last few days of that winter break, but I do know exactly what I did when I got back to school—I put a stop to the late-night pizzas and ate a lot of turkey sandwiches for lunch.

And I walked.

I walked from my dorm to the far end of campus and back— just under four miles. I walked by myself. No friends, no music, no podcasts. Just me and my thoughts. Mile by mile, I felt my brain settle down and my thoughts become clearer.

Here's what happened during that spring semester: I lost the 30-plus pounds I had gained. I made the Dean's List. I helped to found a new chapter of a national sorority with 18 other amazing women. I switched my major from dance to business.

In short, I found my footing.

Fast Forward to 35

My son was born at 7:35 p.m. via emergency c-section. It had been a typical labor until the doctor discovered the baby was breech and his heart rate was plummeting. The labor room catapulted into action, my "birth plan" was tossed out the window, and I was rushed into surgery.

Four days later I was home with a new baby, another 40-pound weight gain, and an incision that stretched clear across my abdomen. I found recovery very, very hard. I remember calling my friend Judi, a veteran of two c-sections, and crying, "When does it stop hurting?"

"Soon," she promised. "Soon."

And my husband and I? Holding on by a thread. We were co-parenting, but not connecting.

A few weeks later, we woke to bright, brilliant sunshine, a rarity in New York in February. Feeling brave and desperate for fresh air, we bundled the baby up, placed him carefully in the stroller, and headed out for a walk. I can still feel the sun on my face and the handle of the stroller. And I can picture the hideous yellow maternity jacket, which was still the only thing that fit.

I recall, with absolute clarity, turning to my husband and saying, *I think we can do this*. And that was the turning point.

Then There was British Columbia

Our first business failed spectacularly. Within weeks of being married, we had quit our jobs, sold our apartment, and put everything into our new business. And then we lost it all—our entire savings, the money from the sale of the apartment, and even the money we had borrowed from our families.

We had no choice but to pick ourselves up, dust ourselves off, and start over again. And we had, believing this time would be different.

Yet, here we were, four years into business No. 2, with baby No. 2 on the horizon, and things were once again shaky.

We had struck a bad deal with our partner. The business wasn't growing. We struggled to make payroll—I had four of my own paychecks tucked in my desk drawer, uncashed—there wasn't enough money in the bank to cover them.

We were in trouble.

Again.

In light of all of that, I don't have any idea how or why I decided that that was the time to head to British Columbia to go hiking for a week—by myself. I don't remember where the money for the trip came from, or why Eric agreed it was a good time for me to disappear for a week—leaving him to manage both our business and our family.

But that's what I did. I spent a week hiking with ten strangers. We hiked six hours a day and when we weren't hiking we were massaging our sore feet, sleeping, or eating.

On the last morning, I walked a mile to a stream by myself, tossed pebbles into the flowing water, and had an idea. It was the synthesis of many things I'd been thinking about. My two kids were young. We lived in a thriving community that offered so many enriching events and activities for kids and families. But, even as an involved mom, I sometimes missed the best storytimes and family fun days. As I tossed those pebbles into the water, I thought: *What if we created a weekly email for local parents that shared all of the family-friendly events and activities in our community?*

I didn't know where the idea would go. I didn't know what it would be called. But I knew, standing beside that stream in British Columbia having walked more than seventy-five miles over the past week, I was onto something.

That idea would ultimately become Macaroni Kid, a multi-million dollar media company that publishes hundreds of local Macaroni Kid editions all over the United States, enriching communities and reaching more than three million families each week.

Are you noticing a theme? Me too. Throughout my life I have processed big things, found my footing, created my best ideas, and gotten a handle on my weight and well-being by putting one foot in front of the other. Walking has saved me more times than I can count.

And I know I'm not alone.

Yup, Walking is Magic

I began thinking about the impact walking has had throughout my life. Curious, I started researching. We all know that walking is good for us, but how good?

So, so good. Walking can transform your body and add years to your life. It can improve your cardiovascular health and reduce your risk of high blood pressure, diabetes, and several types of cancer. Walking can support weight loss, strengthen your bones, reduce your risk of dementia, and actually make your brain bigger.

In fact, walking is so good for your body that one study showed that just 20-25 minutes of intentional, brisk walking daily can add up to seven years to your life. Seven years!

And your mind? Studies have shown that walking fuels creativity, lifts moods, combats depression, improves focus, and boosts decision-making.

Honestly, I could go on and on. There are thousands of studies on the benefits of walking.

But there's more. Have you ever said, "I come up with my best ideas while I'm walking?"

You're not wrong. Research has proven that our brains process differently while we walk, so it's no surprise that history's greatest and most innovative thinkers—including Beethoven, Aristotle, Einstein, Darwin, and Jobs took long walks while they considered, created, and innovated.

Walking creates the ideal environment for your best thinking.

The Last Piece of the Puzzle: Loneliness, Guilt and the Pressure to be Perfect

During the past decade, I've spent hundreds of hours working with women helping them rediscover their dreams, crush their goals, and manage the inevitable challenges and frustrations. I've heard over and over from women who sacrifice tremendous parts of themselves in pursuit of "perfect motherhood" or strive to achieve some vision of perfection, obsessing about everything from their social media engagement to the arch of their eyebrows.

I've heard about mom guilt and a litany of reasons why women don't believe they can, or should, take care of themselves. I've heard defeat in their voices as they talk about the dreams they've abandoned and all of the reasons why every diet has failed them.

In early 2019, we undertook a study called "The State of Mom." 2,300 women responded to our survey. While the results shouldn't have surprised me, to see it laid out in black and white is still a bit startling. Among the discoveries we made:

- 90% of moms feel that they take better care of their families than they do of themselves.
- 22% can't even remember the last time they did something for themselves.
- 45% feel as though they don't have enough time for their friends, and 17% don't feel they have time to even have friends.
- 52% sometimes feel lonely, while a whopping 21% feel lonely "most" of the time.
- Pretty much everyone—90%—are unhappy with their weight.

That's a lot of unhappy, unfulfilled, stressed, lonely women.

Here's what I know. We all want to be happier. We all want to live longer. We all want to be more creative. We all want to improve our focus and our creativity. And most of us want to lose some weight.

That's where this book comes in.

This Book

This is not a book about losing weight, although adopting a regular walking practice can help you do that. This is not a book about improving your mood or helping combat depression, although adopting a regular walking practice can do that. This is not a book about becoming a more patient parent or becoming happier, although adopting a regular walking practice can do that. This is not a book about reversing early stage diabetes, strengthening your bones, or making your brain bigger or your heart stronger, although adopting a regular walking practice can do that too.

This is a book about walking your way to better.

Each section provides a thought-starter, a piece of information, a story, or research that I think is important. But I don't want you to just read it. I want you to read a section and then lace up your sneakers and head out the door because while walking, your brain will process information in a unique way. When you finish the walk, take a moment to capture a few thoughts right away. If you don't, the insights and ideas will disappear the same way a dream is lost if you don't capture it right when you wake up. I know, we are all busy—we're going to talk a lot about how busy we are—but capture the thoughts anyway. I promise—it will take you less than five minutes.

Now go grab a notebook or pad of paper. Or, better yet, take notes in the margin, underline the things that seem important, make lists right in this book. Doodle. Draw smiley faces. Fill the empty spaces with the answers to the questions I pose and the things you think about.

Read, walk, process, write, and bit by bit, become better.

Don't worry if you don't remember everything you thought about during your walk. Don't worry if your mind wandered. Your brilliant brain will hold onto the things you need most and the thoughts will be there, percolating.

Not every section will resonate with you. Not every section is what you need to hear. But I promise you this: there will be at least two dozen that have the power to transform your life.

Join me on this journey as we walk our way to better.

● ● ●

Walk # 1: Let's Begin

"A journey of a thousand miles begins with a single step."
— Laozi

Let's begin. Let's make today the day you start taking the steps you need to become the person you want to be and to live the life you want to live. We are going to clear the clutter, silence the negative voices, and put one step in front of the other.

Nope, it won't be easy.

We wake up every day to an onslaught of obligations. Babies wake (often ridiculously early) and need to be fed and loved and changed. Kids need to be woken (often repeatedly) and fed and loved and readied for school. Dogs need to be walked. Partners need to be greeted with a kind word or two. And, of course, coffee needs to be brewed, lunches need to be packed, showers need to be taken, beds need to be made, and, for many of us, all of those things need to happen before 7 a.m.

And then there are the habits we have and the way we do the things we do. Same habits, some results. You know the cliché: if you want what you've always had, do what you've always done. If you want something different, you'll have to do something different.

Like I said, this won't be easy. As you begin to make changes and move toward your better self and better life, your patterns, habits, and obligations will get in the way. Your daily whirlwind will pull you back. There might be people in your life who, even though they love you—or maybe because they love you—won't want you to change. There will be voices in your head sowing doubt and fear and negativity.

We will learn to ignore those voices. We will learn to fight the whirlwind. We will practice saying, *"Thank you for caring, and I know change is hard, but this is what I want and need to do."*

Now, understand that what your better life looks like is going to be very different from what my better life looks like. And it will be different than what your neighbor Carla's better life looks like. It might be different from what your parents, partner, or children think your better life should look like.

Your dad, like my dad, might not want you to walk away from your legal career.

Your mom might want you to go back to school to finish that accounting degree.

Your kids might not want you to do anything that takes even a second of your attention away from them.

Your partner might be afraid of what your growth means for them.

How will we handle it?

We will talk about why change is hard, and we will work through 99 steps to change your life for the better. But for today, let's begin by thinking about what we truly want. Because before we start striding down the path of how to make life better, we need to be sure that path is leading someplace we actually want to go.

There are two things to be mindful of as you begin this journey.

First, this works only if you are honest. Deeply, completely, and totally honest. With yourself. No one is going to hear the thoughts in your head—or see the notes you capture as you read this book—but you. No one.

Second, embrace the fact that what you want and what is most important to you right now might be very different than what you want in five, ten, or fifteen years. That's okay. This is an exercise in becoming mindful of your priorities, dreams, and goals—*right now*.

Now is the time to begin to dream. Picture yourself this time next year and let your fantasy take over. What does the dream life look like? What do you do during the day? Where do you live? Who do you surround yourself with? What do you learn? What do you create? How much money is in the bank? How do you feel when you wake up each morning?

Now picture yourself ten years from now. What do you do during the day? Where do you live? Who do you surround yourself with? What do you learn? What do you create? How much money is in the bank? How do you feel when you wake up each morning?

Consider dreams you have postponed. Are there activities that give you joy that you no longer "have time" for? Are there people in your life who feed your spirit who you no longer "have time" for?

For many of us, dreaming can feel super risky. We've been told that being a mom is the most important and fulfilling job in the world, so you may wonder, *am I disrespecting my kids and my motherhood by wanting more?* We've learned hard lessons from failure and disappointment. We've been told to grow up. We've filled our lives to the breaking point with things that keep us so, so busy that we convince ourselves that we no longer have time for big dreams.

On today's walk, indulge in the fantasy of that life one year from now and ten years from now. Explore not just what you do in that dream life, but how you feel in that life. Your energy, your heart.

When you get back, spend a few minutes capturing those thoughts on a piece of paper, the margin below, or in a fresh notebook. No editing. No second-guessing. Just describe the life you want.

Walk # 2: Let's Keep Dreaming, Bigger This Time

When I was pregnant with my first, well-meaning people would say, "Get ready, your whole life is about to change."

Then my son was born and we began to find a new normal. While I suddenly had many more responsibilities, and much less sleep, my life didn't seem to change a whole lot. I was still me. I remember one winter evening when we had to get out of the house. My husband, Eric, wanted to go to the movies.

"That's impossible," I said.

But he convinced me with a promise that if the baby started to cry, we'd leave. So off we went. We bought a huge bucket of popcorn and I nursed the baby during the previews. He quickly fell asleep and slept soundly through the entire movie and all the way home. I remember thinking, *We can go to the movies! Nothing has changed.*

But I was wrong, and those well-meaning people were right—in fact, everything had changed, I just didn't know it yet. Not because my time was now absorbed by the baby—even though that was true—but because my priorities had changed, even if I didn't see it happening. Once we step into motherhood, we begin to make choices based on what we believe will be best for someone else. And we do it out of such a deep well of love that it can shatter our sense of self and potentially destroy our ability to make choices that will be best for *ourselves.*

Here's the thing: we are still entitled to our dreams. We deserve the very best life and need to realize that our dreams and what is best for our families are not mutually exclusive. And we need to know that pursuing our dreams is *not* selfish. In fact, the opposite is true: Pursuing our own dreams is life-affirming and sets an important example for our children.

My friend Karen is incredibly smart, creative, and talented. She's also the mom of two—a daughter she is homeschooling and a toddler with special needs. Karen had surrendered herself to doing everything for her two children and nothing for herself. Her self-neglect eventually landed her in the emergency room, where she discovered a blown disc in her back, and a frightening heart problem.

"I don't ever prioritize myself," she told me. "I know that, but I can't seem to help it."

Karen loves her daughter fiercely. She wants only the best for her.

"So, let me ask you a question," I asked her. "Picture your daughter twenty years from now as a young mom with two kids. Would you want her to live the way you are living?"

"No," she said. "No," she repeated.

"What would you want for her?"

"I'd want her to be fulfilled and happy, and I'd want her to take care of herself."

"Does the version of motherhood you are modeling, what you are showing her, give her the best chance at that?"

"No," she said. "I would never want her to neglect herself like I have or to feel how I feel."

You deserve your dreams. You deserve your life. If you won't do it for yourself, do it because going after what's important to you and creating a life that is fulfilling shows your children a path to follow so they can chase their own dreams. Living in closer alignment with your dreams will bring more joy to your family and home. And it will make you healthier and potentially enable you to live longer.

Convinced? Good, then let's begin by thinking about how to align your life with your dreams.

"I want to be an astronaut."

"I want to be a veterinarian."

These seem to be two of the top career choices for six-year-olds. Why an astronaut or a veterinarian? Because at six, children have a sense of wonder about the world and their place in it. Everything feels fresh and possible.

By the time these same six-year-olds reach high school, they replace those dream careers with "I need to earn a living" or "make a lot of money" at the top of their lists.

Why?

Because we teach them those priorities and values.

Sure, earning enough money to live comfortably is important, but living a life that aligns with your personal values and your biggest dreams is equally as important. Maybe even more important.

So... what were your six-year-old dreams? What gave you a spark of joy when you were a kid? What dreams are still lying dormant in your heart? Is it opening a baking school? Writing a book? Visiting Venice?

Learning to paint? Living by the beach? Skiing thirty days next winter? Or is it quitting your job to be home while your kids are young?

Recognizing your dream is mission-critical. Every day things will happen to pull you off course. Sometimes doors open along the way and you will walk through them because the opportunity seemed too good to pass up. Yet years later, you look back and realize that what seemed an "opportunity" actually didn't align with what you really, *really* wanted and threw you off your course.

On our last walk, you pictured your dream life. On today's walk, free yourself to dream a really, really big dream. Take it beyond the reasonable dream. Go big. Really big. Yup, this is scary. There will be a voice inside your head that says, "that's impossible" or "that's too big" or "that's not realistic" or "what if...." Ignore those voices and, just for fun, on today's walk, go ahead and dream a big dream. When you get back, spend a few minutes capturing that dream in the margin below or in your new notebook.

● ● ●

Walk # 3: Lessons from the Bathroom Floor

It was 2:00 a.m. on a random weekday in 2007. My kids were two and seven and sleeping soundly. My husband was traveling, and my list for the following day was long. I was lying on the bathroom floor with a stomach bug. Not just any stomach bug. *The* stomach bug. The one that keeps you lying on the bathroom floor trying to figure out how you are possibly going to survive it.

By morning, the eye of the storm had passed. I was off the cold tile floor and in my warm bed, where I would remain for the better part of the next two days, drinking tea and eating the occasional piece of toast. On my calendar for the week were two full days of meetings, one writing deadline, a dinner for a women's networking group that *I* had created, a meeting with my daughter's teacher, and two playdates. Everything got canceled. Every single thing. My kids had Lunchables for lunch (without the obligatory added apple) and instant oatmeal for dinner.

And you know what? Nothing terrible happened. Because—and I know this might be hard to hear—we are not indispensable, and certainly not for a couple of days.

Yet we don't stop until we are forced to stop. We don't make time for ourselves until illness forces us to slow down. "Sick is the new vacation for moms," a therapist once told me. She's absolutely right. We keep going until we break down. We keep pushing until our bodies have had enough. We say "yes" until our bodies say "no." When we recover, we are so grateful to feel better that we immediately jump back into our lives with a vengeance to make up for the things we didn't do while we were sick. We don't learn the lesson. We continue to fill every possible moment of our day. We still complicate everything.

Gone are the days where you could learn your job, perfect your performance, and replicate it. Today our jobs are more complex and our responsibilities shift daily. The pressure is on to constantly innovate, build a team, or lead an army. We strive to parent perfectly, even though what that means changes weekly. In the palm of our hands—pretty much at all times—we hold enough news, social media, television, movies, magazines, blog posts, videos, podcasts, and games to keep us busy for eternity.

Everywhere we look—including in the pages of this book—we are being encouraged to dream bigger, work harder, and accomplish more. We fill our days to the breaking point.

Now here's the dirty little secret—the truth. *You* are the one who filled your days to the breaking point. *You* are the one who said "yes" when you should have said "no." *You* are the one who lost track of the things that are important to you. *You* are the one who allowed the remarkable device in your hand to consume millions of the precious moments of your life.

So, if you are reading this book and thinking, *I don't have thirty minutes to walk and ponder important questions and begin to make changes in my life*, let me be frank: yes, you do. Yes, it will mean making choices. Different choices. It might mean going outside when it is drizzling. It might mean making dinner in the crockpot. It might mean asking your partner to, well, be a partner and hold down the fort while you take thirty minutes for yourself. It might mean the laundry waits until tomorrow. It might mean you get out of bed thirty minutes earlier, go to bed thirty minutes earlier, or forsake social media on those days when you have committed to reading and walking.

You can find thirty minutes in your day that you can claim to do something for your body, heart, mind, and spirit. So make it a priority.

For today's exercise (no pun intended) write down everything you can think of that can help you reclaim fifteen minutes. Everything that can be skipped—not every day, but some days. For instance:

- I typically spend about thirty minutes a day on social media. I love social media and don't want to give it up, but I could set a timer and spend only fifteen minutes on the days that I commit to walking.

- I can get up fifteen minutes earlier and take a fifteen-minute walk before the kids get up.

- I can get off the subway two stops earlier and walk fifteen minutes to the office.

- I can plan two crockpot dinners each week and walk fifteen minutes before dinner.

Everyone's life is different, and everyone has different windows of time and opportunity. But those opportunities *are there* for you. It's up to you to find them.

On today's walk, think about the places in your life where you can make those opportunities happen. Some may be things you can do daily, like getting up fifteen minutes earlier, while others might be things you can do once a week, like walking while your daughter is in gymnastics class. When you get back, create a list titled "15 Minutes for Me."

● ● ●

Walk # 4: What I Learned from Double Unders

"Jump higher."

"Keep your feet closer together."

"Turn the rope faster."

"Practice every day."

"Focus on a spot on the wall."

"That rope's too long for you."

"That rope's too short for you."

"Relax and find your rhythm."

"Don't hold your breath."

"Practice slowing the rope down and speeding it up."

"Take the same number of warm-up jumps every time."

These are just some examples of the advice I've been given during the five-plus years that I've struggled to master the "double under," a classic CrossFit exercise where a jump rope passes beneath your feet twice each time you jump. Jump high, spin fast.

In order to successfully complete even a single double under, the rope must move very quickly, so most people don't use a traditional jump rope. Instead, they use a jump rope made from a skinny wire coated with a thin layer of plastic. While struggling to learn double unders, you get struck by that wire a lot. Across your shoulders, your hands, your arms, and the tips of your toes. Often when you miss—which I've done literally thousands of times—those welts will remain for the better part of a day or two.

We all have skills we need to develop to become the person we strive to be. Often, acquiring those skills takes time, consistency, and perseverance. Sometimes, acquiring those skills leaves proverbial welts in the form of failures, challenges, and frustrations.

As of the time of this writing, I linked eleven double unders for the first time. Yesterday, I was only able to do six. But tomorrow, I plan to do twelve.

Think about the skills you need to use or develop in order to accomplish the goals you have set for yourself. For instance, if you want to advance your position at work—perhaps by mastering Excel, becoming a great public speaker, or acquiring a new language—learning and incorporating these skills will fill your arsenal. If you want to feed your family better, perhaps you need to improve at meal planning or become better educated about nutrition. If you want to improve your fitness, lose weight, have a richer and more fulfilling relationship, or yell at your kids less, there are skills that you can work on that will advance each of those. And if you want to be a better CrossFit athlete, you need to master double unders.

It is likely that right this second you are struggling with some—or perhaps most—of those skills. That's okay. Growth, improvement, and change are what make life a beautiful challenge.

As you walk today, settle your mind on one skill you want to develop or improve upon. Picture yourself having mastered that skill. Envision yourself standing in front of a group of co-workers confidently giving a presentation, getting the kids out the door in the morning without raising your voice, or walking hand-in-hand with your partner down the street.

Next, consider your available resources. We live in an age in which the world's best thought leaders offer their insights freely. Whatever skill you seek to improve, there are books, blogs, articles, podcasts, and videos to help you. Make a mental list of all the places you can seek help, encouragement, and advice.

Picture the person you want to be. Identify a key skill that person has mastered. Keep that person in your mind and work on that skill over time. Yup, it might take five years to get that damn rope to pass twice beneath your feet when you jump. And it might take another two years before you can link 30 double unders at will. But if you don't see what you want to accomplish or open your mind to the resources that can help you—and then work toward it consistently—you will never get there. So, start today.

Walk # 5: Beware the Voices in Your Head

We all have voices in our heads. Sometimes those voices tell us we aren't good enough to have the life that we want. Sometimes those voices remind us that we have tried before and failed, and they ask—and not in a very nice way—*what in the world makes us think this time will be different*? Sometimes those voices tell us that the risks are too great. Sometimes those voices tell us that wanting more is selfish and greedy.

Where do those voices come from?

First, they come from experience. When we were young, the world seemed like a place of boundless opportunity and limitless magic. How can you not believe in boundless opportunity and limitless magic when your first tooth is taken by a mysterious fairy who leaves you a shiny quarter, or when a jolly man sneaks into your house to give you everything your four-year-old heart desires? But then experience comes crashing down on those beliefs. We fail. People we trust betray us. The horrors of the world hit our newsfeed daily. We learn that not all risks pay off and not all dreams come true.

Second, the voices in our heads are hard-wired. Beyond the confines of our distant ancestor's caves lurked all kinds of dangers. Beyond our closest family group were people bent on our destruction. When winter came, food all but disappeared, so we needed to eat up while we could. Straying from our own well-worn path was dangerous. The risk was too risky. Those voices in our heads were placed there to keep us safe from dangers that no longer exist, yet those voices persist.

Finally, some of those voices were instilled by our parents. Here's how I got mine. Thirty years ago, my parents sold our family home and moved to Florida. When I was expecting my first child, my dad ran into a neighbor and told him how excited he was to have a grandchild on the way.

"Congratulations," the neighbor said. "We've got three up in New York and we get to see them a couple of times a year."

A couple of times a year? My dad was horrified at the prospect of not being a meaningful part of his grandkid's life. So my parents bought a small condo ten minutes from our home. This was the start of two decades of a "grass is always greener" struggle. Here's how it went. Whenever he was in Florida—which was most of the time—my father longed to be in New York with the family. But whenever he was in New York—away from the comforts, routines, and familiarity of his primary home—he wanted to be in Florida. While at home in Florida, he would speak wistfully about missing us and wanting to come up to visit. Within days of arriving in New York, he inevitably began grumbling about going home. For my dad, there was always someplace better.

I inherited that voice. That is the voice in my head. The voice that says, "But wait, you should be doing something else. This is a waste of time. You have committed to the wrong project, chosen the wrong path, taken a wrong turn. There is something more important you should be doing or a more valuable contribution you should be making."

Perhaps some of you inherited whispering voices telling you that you are not good enough, not smart enough, not young enough, or not thin enough. Someone told you these things and maybe, just maybe, you began to believe them.

Today as you walk, think about the negative voices in your head that hold you back. Identify the phrases you hear most often and think about where they came from: experience, biology, your family, or someplace else? Don't worry, we are going to work on ways to quiet the voices that hold you back and amplify the voices that propel you forward. But before we can tell them to stop, we need to hear them. When you get back from your walk, write down what those voices tell you. Nope, this won't be fun. Do it anyway.

Walk # 6: Feed the Good Wolf

On our last walk, we worked on hearing the negative voices in our heads. Today, we will work on amplifying the voices that encourage us to be the best version of ourselves and quiet the voices that spew doubt, fear, and shame.

There is an old story, attributed to the Cherokee, that captures how to do this. It goes something like this.

An elderly grandfather was walking with his grandson through the woods, sharing the wisdom he had gleaned throughout his seventy-three years. "Within us," he said, "are two wolves locked in a constant state of battle—a good wolf and a bad wolf. The good wolf represents all of the good things we seek to be: brave, honest, true, happy, and generous of spirit. The bad wolf represents greed, anger, selfishness, arrogance, hatred, and fear. Throughout our lives," the man finished, "these two wolves will battle."

The boy looked up at his grandfather and asked, "Which one will win?"

The grandfather replied simply, "Whichever one you feed."

Those wolves represent the voices we all have inside of us. No one is the perfect version of themselves. No one is free from self-doubt or immune to anger and jealousy, and everyone is capable of joy, love, and acts of generosity.

But here's what most of us don't do well. Most of us don't take a step back to look—and I mean really look—at how we are feeding each of our wolves, let alone mindfully seeking out those things that feed the good wolf.

There are people in your life who feed your good wolf: the friends who support you and love you unconditionally, the people who make you laugh, inspire you to grow, and encourage you when you need them. And then there are people in your life who feed the bad wolf by spewing negativity, doubt, and gossip.

It helps to recognize that the people spewing negativity do so because of who *they* are. It has nothing to do with you. Perhaps they are jealous as they watch you taking steps toward a better life. Perhaps they are so lost in their own unhappiness or challenges that they simply don't have the ability to give in a positive way. Perhaps... well, you know what? It doesn't matter. If people in your life feed your bad wolf, you must consciously remind yourself that their issues are their issues and mindfully limit your connection with them. I'm not suggesting that you cut them out of your life entirely—although sometimes that is the best solution. Sometimes those people are members of your family, or your neighbors, or the parents of your child's best friend—in other words, people whom you simply cannot remove from your life completely. But even if you can't remove them from your life, you can refuse to let them offer treats to your bad wolf.

Consider your use of social media. Is it feeding your good wolf or your bad wolf? If you are like me (and, I suspect, most of us) it is feeding both. It is lovely to see my cousin's children growing up in California, exciting to learn about the movie recently produced by an old high school friend, and fun to catch a meme that so perfectly captures my day. Those things feed my good wolf. But my bad wolf is fed by images of perfectly-curated lives that spur jealousy and by "friends" who seem to be doing more—losing more pounds, lifting more weights, enjoying more fabulous vacations, and making more money. For most of us, social media feeds both wolves, and it is on us to consume it both carefully and thoughtfully. We'll explore the impact of social media further in our next walk, but for now, consider how you spend your valuable time and what you prioritize.

Here's a secret: your good wolf loves to be outside—in nature. She loves to move and stretch and grow. She loves fresh food and sunshine. She loves to play. She loves hard work. She loves her pack. She loves to be with people who bring her joy. She loves to care for her pups. She loves a den that is cozy, safe, and warm.

On today's walk, think about the two wolves inside of you and consider what you do that feeds the good wolf and what feeds the bad.

● ● ●

Walk # 7: Social Media: Friend or Foe?

On our last walk, we considered how social media can feed both our good wolf and our bad wolf. I thought of that as I opened Facebook this morning to glimpse the lives of old friends and people I barely know. Engagements. Weddings. Anniversaries. Children's birthdays accompanied by elaborate Thomas the Train cakes. Friends and acquaintances sporting bikinis and drinks on beach vacations or in ski pants and parkas atop snow-covered mountains. The occasional political diatribe. Groups of friends celebrating, well, pretty much anything.

Next I went to Instagram. Dogs. Couples walking together. People in places where there's sunshine. Occasional words of inspiration. Countless weight loss struggles and a few promises of miracle products.

Assuming you are among the 75% of American women who spend time on social media, I suspect your feeds look pretty much the same.

Social media enables us to connect in ways we never could before. My dad, who recently turned 90, keeps up with old friends and former students (he's a retired teacher and coach) and loves to see what's happening with family members all across the country. He scrolls through his feed at least once a day and feels far more connected and informed than ever would have been possible without the power of social media. I love to see my cousin's kids growing up in California and share the journey of another friend as she bravely battles cancer. A mom whose son has an extremely rare medical condition has been able to connect with others to share resources, experiences, and the kind of support that can only come from someone who is dealing with the same challenges she is.

Connected. Communicating. Keeping up.

Social media is awesome.

Until it's not.

The evidence is mounting that our unchecked consumption of social media is contributing to feelings of isolation and depression. *Why?* Three reasons:

Wait, where did that hour go? Social media can be a time suck. This is no surprise because the people who design the social media platforms we love have meticulously researched exactly how to keep our attention long after we should have logged off to take a walk or go make dinner. They are deliberately manipulating our attention to keep us from leaving and they are really, really good at it. They strategically tailor our social media feeds precisely to addict us, and they're constantly getting better at it. That means that what should have been just twenty minutes catching up with old friends easily becomes two hours of mindless scrolling. It means we actually can become addicted to social media—because they've effectively designed it way.

Compare and despair. Even though we all know that we are looking at a carefully curated version of our friends' lives, it is all but impossible not to envy their great love stories, big houses, and gorgeous children. You know, logically, that you are only seeing a glimpse of these lives and that everyone's story is filtered, layered, and complicated, and no one's life is perfect. But being confronted with the perfect version of your high school nemesis' life day in and day out? Sheesh! It is so, so easy to compare those moments to the messiness that is our own life, to envy those vacations, to feel like we are not doing enough, earning enough, beautiful enough, or thin enough. Social media is fueled by compare and despair.

But wait, I have hundreds of friends! We are social creatures who are meant to live in a community and nurture close connections. Social media gives us the illusion of having robust, meaningful relationships, but lacks the intimacy that is essential for all of us. Put another way, social media is no substitute for the kind of relationships that can only be built one-on-one and are best built in person.

Social media is both good and bad.

Good in moderation. Good when used to stay connected with people we care about and good when we need to find a group of people with whom we share a common experience.

Bad when it becomes a replacement for meaningful in-person relationships. Bad when we feel ourselves getting caught up in social comparisons. And that's not even addressing the toxic political landscape that often finds its way onto our social media feeds.

On today's walk, while away from social media, think about the ways you consume social media. Is it the first thing you look at in the morning and the last thing you check before bed? Do you have "friends" on Facebook who you know aren't really your friends at all? Why are you scrolling Instagram while waiting in the school pick-up line?

Is social media enhancing your life or making you feel bad? If it is making you feel bad, then change how you consume it. Yup, that simple.

Walk # 8: Kaizen On and
The Story of My Morning Smoothie

A couple of years ago I woke up to find an email with this subject in my inbox:

"This one thing will change your life overnight."

Tempting right? It was impossible to fight the urge to open that email. It is human nature to want a quick and easy fix. We are always looking for that magic bullet or bottle of snake oil.

So, I opened it.

It was from a company promising that their supplements, added to a morning smoothie, would deliver a full day's worth of nutrition, increase my energy, and help me lose weight. Too good to be true.

I didn't order the supplements, but it did get me thinking... *was eating the crust off of my daughter's peanut butter and jelly sandwich the best I could do for my own breakfast? Was there a way to start my day with a dose of better nutrition? What if I created the perfect morning smoothie?* And so I began to experiment.

The next morning I filled my blender with sweetened almond milk, kale, protein powder, two ice cubes, and a frozen banana. It was delicious. I drank that formula for months. But there is a lot of sugar in that sweetened almond milk. What if I swap out the sweetened almond milk for unsweetened? *Yuck.* Okay, what if I go half sweetened and half unsweetened? *Better.* How about I add some beet powder and chia seeds? Three ice cubes? A handful of spinach? A slice of avocado (you have to trust me on this, it makes the smoothie incredibly creamy with no weird avocado flavor). Frozen blueberries? A slice of fresh ginger?

Bit by bit, I found my energy was more stable throughout the day. I lost a few pounds. My skin looked healthier. Overall, I felt better.

My morning smoothie has remained a work in progress for the past two years. My kitchen is a constant laboratory for experimentation and improvement. But here's the thing: I don't change it every day. By giving each formula time to have an impact, I learn more about the process.

Whatever my current formula is, that is what I make. I have all of the ingredients in one drawer in the fridge. I can create the current version of my morning smoothie with little thought. It is not about creating something unique each day. It is about tinkering from time to time as I learn more about what might make it better, healthier, and more delicious.

My morning smoothie is a microcosm of the practice of kaizen, a Japanese business philosophy which focuses on continuous, incremental improvement. Its two symbols mean "change" and "good."

Make good changes. Iterate. Improve. Remember that nothing is finished, nothing is complete, nothing is carved in stone, and everything can become better.

Today, let's be on the lookout for areas in our lives where we can begin to make incremental improvements. Here are seven ideas to get you thinking this way, but—and this is important—do not seek to do all of them. Do not let your quest for incremental improvement become yet another overwhelming to-do list.

- If you want to live in a tidier home, begin by making your bed each morning or putting the dishes in the dishwasher right away.
- If you want to improve your eating habits, replace your afternoon bag of chips with an apple.
- If you want to be more present with your family, put your phone in another room for one hour a day.
- If you want to save money, bring lunch to work on Fridays.
- If you want to improve your fitness, park your car on the far side of the parking lot.
- If you want to improve your relationship with your partner, stop what you are doing when they walk in the house and offer a kind word.

None of these things, standing on their own, will change your life overnight. But each presents an opportunity to take an incremental step toward living the life you want. Let's stop looking for the instant fix, embrace the journey, and accept that any meaningful change comes as the result of a thousand small changes. Ignore the shortcuts that promise instant success and instead commit to continuous and incremental improvement.

On today's walk, think about just one or two areas of your life where you'd like to see improvement and then decide on one small change you can make toward improving them. Again, beware of the urge to want to change everything. Rather, understand that you are starting on a journey toward consistent improvements, one step at a time.

Kaizen on and get better every day.

● ● ●

Walk # 9: The Cycle of Doom

My beloved dog collapsed after a two-mile walk on our favorite trail, a two-mile dirt road that ends at a beautiful bay beach. It was a walk we'd done a hundred times together. He had been fine up until that morning. Slowing down a bit, but it was to be expected at his age—he had been getting around well on three legs for eleven years following a nearly catastrophic incident with a car when he was a puppy. But that day, an x-ray quickly revealed the problem: a large tumor in his abdomen that had already spread to his lungs. It was inoperable and the vet suggested we take him home and feed him all of the roasted chicken he wanted. We were devastated.

The next day, we got the dreaded call from the school nurse: please come pick up your son. By 7:00 o'clock that evening, his fever was 103°.

It was February in New York and we hadn't seen the sun for days. Between the sick kid and the sick dog, sleep eluded me. I was depleted and tired.

Feelings of joy? Not so much.

So began the cycle. I started my days with more coffee than usual, which seemed to wake me up a bit, but left me jittery. I was trapped at home, trying to sneak in moments of productive work between fetching soup for my son and hiding medication in meatballs for my dog.

More sleepless nights. More coffee. *Maybe a donut will perk me up? Maybe a second donut will help?* By day four, my energy was tapped out and my mood was worse. I was sad, snappy, and so, so tired.

I was trapped in the cycle of doom:

- Less joy = less energy.
- Less energy = less ability to do things that create joy.
- Less joy = less energy.

Do you see where I'm going with this?

All of us have times in our lives—seasons, if you will—when life doesn't hand us joy. In fact, we have lots of moments. In those moments, we have two choices. Either submit to the misery or work for the joy.

Now I know that some of you are tempted right this moment to throw this book against the wall, to shout at me, "My kid has the flu, my best friend just moved to Florida, my daughter was diagnosed with ADHD, my husband cheated on me, money is tight, the baby is colicky..."—and a whole litany of all of the challenges facing you right now, but stay with me here.

Believe it or not, a boatload of research has shown that you actually have far more control over your emotions than you might think. You can choose to focus on the positive. You can actively work to find windows of gratitude. You can will yourself to take steps to do things that bring you joy—even in the midst of tremendous challenges.

But here's why I believe most of us find it so difficult to do that: GUILT.

How can you possibly choose to experience joy when your son is lying in bed miserable with the flu? How can you choose to enjoy an afternoon of fun when your next mortgage payment is uncertain? How can you choose to be happy when you are grieving?

I get that.

But—and here's the paradox—you will do a far, far better job taking care of the people who need you if you can find a way to tap into feelings of joy and gratitude. If you can find even the smallest window of opportunity to do something that gives you joy, fuels your spirit, and disrupts the cycle of doom, it will help create the energy you need to do your best work in all facets of your life. Parenting. Partnering. Working. This is not easy. This requires that you do two things—both of which are incredibly difficult, but they can be done.

First, despite all that is going on around you and all of the negative draws on your energy, you need to take control of your emotions and force yourself to focus on the positive. This is an act of your will. Grab a pen and a piece of paper and write down three positive things in your life. Take a walk, call a girlfriend, or soak in a bath.

Second—and this is even harder—accept that finding even small pockets of joy and thinking positive thoughts *will* help to fuel the energy you need to do what needs to be done. Give yourself permission to think positive thoughts and experience joy, despite the challenges surrounding you.

On today's walk, think about the things that give you energy and fuel your spirit.

Walk # 10: The Best Parenting Advice I Ever Got

My son was three years old, and I loved him more than I ever imagined possible. He was easy-going, inquisitive, and full of life and energy. Should the situation have arisen, I would have gladly stepped in front of a moving train to save him.

My husband and I are addicted skiers. The sight of snow-covered pine trees, the physical challenge of navigating a steep run, and that feeling when you put your skis on edge and carve a turn brings me unspeakable joy. It is also one of the things that my husband and I love most to do together. We "courted" on the side of a mountain and got engaged in front of a fire at a ski lodge. We've planned businesses on chairlifts and laughed amidst deep piles of snow following particularly spectacular falls.

However, having a three-year-old and being addicted skiers didn't blend very well. But we were trying. Trying to capture a little bit of that pre-child fun, trying to reconnect with ourselves and each other. So off we went to Vermont with a plan to check our son into daycare and spend the day together on the mountain. The destination was a ski resort that promoted itself as a family mountain, so I assumed that the daycare would be warm, welcoming, and enriching.

It wasn't.

Not only was it in the basement, but the lighting was dim, and the three-year-olds were contained in a relatively small gated area. It wasn't unsafe, but it didn't look like it was going to be particularly fun, and it certainly didn't look like it was going to be enriching.

However, we had purchased lift tickets, were dressed to ski, and the sun was shining. So, we left him.

Oh, the guilt! He was fine and seemed none the worse for the day... but oh, the guilt! The next day I was talking to my dad, who has a truly remarkable understanding of people in general and kids in particular. His insights and advice are always spot on and often profound. Here's what he said when I told him how awful I felt:

"You know, you don't do your kids any favors by making sure every experience they have is perfect."

Whoa.

Of course, he's right. We want our kids to be resilient. We want to raise them to be resourceful and independent, and those skills are developed through all types of experiences, both good and bad. They will only learn how to get up again and again if we let them fall down in the first place. They will only learn that people leave and come back if we, well, leave and come back.

Looking back, I have two very distinct memories from that day. The first is of my son standing by the gate looking up at me as my husband and I left to ski. That's the singular memory that sums up all of the mom guilt I've ever felt. But I also remember sitting outside in the sunshine, leaning back against my husband, his arm around me. We had just finished lunch and were taking in a few minutes of sunshine before heading back for a few more runs. I remember feeling more connected with him than I had in months, and more myself than I had in years. I literally remember taking a deep breath and feeling the tension leave my body.

The lesson is two-fold.

First, you deserve to do things that you love to do, that make you who you are, that fill your cup. You deserve joy, pleasure, fun, and happiness. The truth is you did not forfeit your right to those things when you became a mother.

Second, you have the right to do those things even if it means your family and your children make some sacrifices because—and here's the rub—there are valuable lessons to be learned when not every experience your child has is perfect. When they are not living a perfectly curated life.

On today's walk, think about the people you want your children to be. How do you want them to walk through their lives? What lessons do you want to teach them? We should all agree and believe that identifying those things helps us realize that making their lives picture-perfect, smoothing every rough corner, and helping them avoid every frustration and disappointment won't actually help them become the people we most want them to be.

● ● ●

Walk # 11: Be Like Popeye

Popeye the Sailor Man first appeared in a newspaper comic strip in 1929 and later came to life in animated shorts and even later on television. A gruff, muscled guy with an unlit pipe dangling from his lower lip, his great love—Olive Oyl—and a young ward named Swee' Pea. Popeye frequently battled a bully named Bluto and drew strength from eating spinach. His most iconic personal tag line was, "I yam what I yam." Popeye wasn't one to apologize for who he was.

We have a lot to learn from Popeye.

A raft of research has shown that women have a strong propensity to apologize more often than men. Some have speculated that the reason is because women have a lower threshold for what they feel warrants an apology. Others suggest apologizing is a habit, while some argue that men feel they give up power when they apologize, and are therefore far less likely to do so.

While there's no doubt that these things play a role, I believe there's more at work here. Women tend to apologize because we have been told, in thousands of small ways throughout our lives, that our dreams are too big, or our priorities are out of whack. We are told to "put our children first," have careers, and live in beautiful, tidy homes. We are told what our kids and our relationships should look like. We are told we can't have it all while still being fed an endless list of all of the things we are supposed to accomplish, acquire, and achieve.

But what does that mean? If you can't have it all, what are you allowed to have? What can you ask for? What can you expect? What can you strive for? What is the "acceptable" balance between motherhood and being yourself? And most importantly, who is to say? Who has the right to decide what is right for you and your family?

It is time—actually, long past time—for us to embrace who we are and who we want to be. We need to stop apologizing for asking for what we want and striving to design a life that works for us. We need to stop apologizing when we add our opinion to a conversation—how many of us have prefaced our opinion with "I'm sorry, but I think..."?

Do not apologize for what you think. Do not apologize for who you are. *A working mom?* Awesome. *A SAHM?* Great. *A nursing mom?* Have at it. *A bottle-feeding mom?* Good for you. *A skiing mom, a biking mom, a traveling mom, a PTA mom, a bookworm mom*—whatever it is that describes you best.

Say it with me: *"I yam what I yam."*

Now, this is not an excuse to give up on your dreams or to accept the status quo. You should never, ever stop striving to be the fullest expression of the person you were meant to be. Never give up on becoming your very best self or living your very best life. Grow, learn, and get better every day. But all of that work? All of that growth? All of that learning? It should be directed toward the YOU that you want to be.

Embrace your true self and be like Popeye. *"I yam what I yam."* Oh, and eating a lot of spinach, standing up to bullies, and taking care of the people you love? That's good, too.

On today's walk, consider the ways you can be like Popeye. Think about the traits that define you and that are important to you. Own them.

● ● ●

Walk # 12: But Wait! This is Supposed to be Fun!

I called my cousin Jamie a few months after the birth of her first daughter and asked her how it was going. "Everyone tells you that you will be completely overwhelmed by how much you love this little person—and how hard the sleep deprivation is—both of which are true," she said. "But no one tells you how much *fun* it is."

Months later, when I was pregnant with my first child, my friend Nicki, a wise mom of four, told me, "One of the best things about having children is getting the chance to see the world through their eyes." She was right. Your child will stare with wonder at the unique, magical shape of each individual snowflake and you have a choice: share their wonder or rush them inside out of the cold. They will spend an hour trying to teach the dog a new trick. You can join in with your child and dog, or you can sit on the couch and check Facebook. They will create a skyscraper of blocks and clap their hands with excitement as each floor is added. You can help them build it taller, or you can fret about the dust balls you noticed under the couch while you were sitting together on the floor.

I know that some of you are reading this while hiding in the closet, hoping to get through a few pages before a baby wakes from a nap or a toddler comes banging on the door. I know that many of you are sleep deprived, overburdened, and near the end of your rope. I know that several of you have yelled at your kids at some point today—or will before the day is out—and then you will feel guilty and struggle to make it up to them in some way, even though your kids don't keep score. I know a few of you live in fear that you are turning into your mother.

Days with little ones underfoot can be long. Really, really long. There's not a parent among us who has not sometimes counted the hours until the kids go to bed. But I also know that there is not a parent of a kid heading off to college who doesn't stand in awe at how fast it all went by.

"It went in a blink," my friend Helen posted on Facebook just this morning as she celebrated her daughter's 18th birthday.

I promise, your children's childhoods will be gone before you know it, yet the thing you will regret most is not enjoying the journey.

It's not that we don't know this. In 1974, Harry Chapin gave us fair warning when he released the iconic song "Cat's in the Cradle" and warned that if we fill our days with work and put off fun with our kids, we will turn around and find that they are adults with families of their own, destined to repeat our mistakes.

But how? How do you make time for fun when your neighbor, your mother, your children's teachers, and the media bombard you with the message that to be a good mom you must subsume yourself into your child? Your child's successes are your successes and their failures are your failures. Your house must be perfect, and the meals you serve must be organic. Technology is to be feared and managed. Fun is frivolous— certainly, there are more important things to do.

But wait a minute! Fun is not frivolous. Fun is the point! Life is meant to be savored and enjoyed. *Isn't that the lesson we want to teach our children? Don't we, as fully functioning people, deserve fun too?*

On today's walk—which you should take even if your house is messy or the laundry isn't done or if it requires bundling up the baby and putting her in the stroller—think about what things are fun for you. If you had an hour a day during which you were prohibited from accomplishing anything, how would you spend it? What activities did you used to do that were fun? Do you love to ride rollercoasters, knit sweaters, waterski, lay on the beach, read romance novels, do gymnastics, play volleyball, dine out with girlfriends, watch movies, take road trips, or treasure hunt in antique stores? Do you like to refinish furniture, paint with watercolors, or learn new languages?

I know, I know, I know... we are busy. But I promise, there is room to infuse just a little more fun in our lives. And a little more fun leads to a little more fun leads to a little more fun.

On today's walk, think about all of the things that are fun—fun for *you* because what is fun for you might not be what is fun for anyone else. And that's okay. This is your life and this is your list.

● ● ●

Walk # 13: You Won't Fall in Love with the Chinese Delivery Guy

When I was young and single and living in New York City, there was an expression amongst my friends that captured the need to get out and meet someone—and by "someone" we usually meant a guy. When my friend Caroline would call and ask me to join her at a party, I often said no. I had a very demanding job, I am not a night person, and more often than not, I'd rather be home in my PJs with a book. Invariably, she would say, "Well, you won't fall in love with the Chinese delivery guy." She knew that to be lucky in love, you had to get out and meet as many people as possible. As it turned out, it was on one of those Caroline-inspired adventures that I met my husband.

Two years ago, my husband and I were looking for a new office for our business. Our old office building had been sold and the new landlords were... well, let's just say we needed a new office, and fast. We signed a lease on garage space and were scheduled to begin moving in the next day. At 2:00 in the morning, I woke in a panic. The space would not work. There was no parking and no storage. It was too small. Trucks would never be able to make deliveries. It was dark and it was going to be a disaster. We couldn't move in there.

I was panicked.

After a sleepless night, I got up, got dressed, got in my car, and drove to a street that we had always believed would be the perfect location for our office. I went door to door, building to building asking if anyone had 1,000 square feet to rent.

As I pulled into the parking area of THE building we most wanted to move into, I saw a man locking the door of one of the offices. I hopped out of my car.

"Excuse me," I said. "We are looking for an office here and I wondered if you know of anyone who might be moving out."

The man stopped mid-turn of his key and looked at me. "Wow," he said. "I really need to move out of this space, but I'm locked into a lease. The landlord said she'd let me out if I could find someone to take it."

We moved in sixty days later. We were so lucky.

Or were we?

Many years ago, I read about a study of luck. Or, I should say, about what people believe about their own "luckiness" and how that impacts the way in which they move through the world.

I don't remember all of the details, but it went something like this. The researchers selected two groups of people, one group that self-identified as "lucky" and one group that self-identified as "unlucky." They put the two groups in identical situations in the "real world." In one situation, the subjects were seated in a diner beside someone who could be extremely helpful to their career. In another, the researchers simply placed $5 bills in their paths.

Here's what the study revealed. Those people who believed that they were lucky discovered the helpful person sitting beside them in the diner and also found the $5 laying their path. Those who considered themselves unlucky didn't meet the person or find the money.

Those findings are consistent with those of Richard Wiseman, who is credited with taking on the largest academic research project into luck (aptly named "The Luck Project"). Years of research with hundreds of participants led to insights into how people "create" their own luck. He observed four tendencies of "lucky" people.

First, "lucky" people tend to embrace chance encounters. You never know who you're going to end up talking to, just like the lucky woman at the diner who struck up a conversation with the woman sitting next to her or the chance I took when I approached the man outside that office.

Second, "lucky" people are open to new experiences, expanding their horizons, and trying new things. They deliberately take steps to introduce new experiences into their lives, sometimes by simple things such as varying their route to work.

Third, "lucky" people anticipate positive outcomes—they tend to be more optimistic. When faced with a new situation or a fresh challenge, they envision that things will go as they hope and focus less on the risks, dangers, or potential downside.

Fourth, "lucky" people tend to look up and not down, literally and figuratively. They keep a broad horizon and are open to people, information, and opportunities, especially those that might not be what they thought they were looking for.

Sure, no amount of keeping your eyes open or anticipating a positive outcome will help you win the lottery. But research suggests that a big part of luck is keeping your eyes and options open. To believe that this is a world of opportunities—not roadblocks. To connect with those around you. To believe in yourself, your abilities, and the possibility of good fortune.

On today's walk, take a different route and, if the opportunity presents itself, say hello to the people you meet along the way.

Walk # 14: Consider Rebecca

I've known Rebecca for close to a decade. When we first met, she was in the midst of raising four kids, working part-time, and battling a chronic medical condition. She buzzed with anxiety. Her worries had worries and she talked a-mile-a-minute, barely pausing for a breath. She was the queen of "what if"—*what if this bad thing happens? Or that bad thing happens?*

One fall Rebecca and I traveled together to a work conference. Along with five colleagues, we stole an afternoon to visit a spa near the conference's hotel. As we lay on chaise lounges with cucumbers on our eyes, amazed by her obvious transformation, I finally said what I'd been thinking all weekend. "Rebecca, you're a completely different person."

"I know," she replied.

"Can I ask what happened?"

"I woke up and realized that if I didn't change everything, I was going to die. Literally."

Intrigued, I pressed for more details.

"Was there a specific moment when you realized things had to change?"

"Yup, there was a morning. But it was kinda a morning like most other mornings—challenging and stressful but nothing really crazy or out of the ordinary. I got the kids up and out the door for school, sat down with my third cup of coffee, and noticed that I had zero energy. Like, zero. As in I had no idea how I was going to push through the day.

"I sat there and looked at my life, and I just had this moment when I realized that if I kept going like that, well...it wasn't going to be good."

Every story of true transformation or meaningful change starts with a moment like that. When I stepped on the scale over winter break of my sophomore year in college and discovered that I had added more than 30 pounds to my slight 5'3" frame. When my friend Karen fell out of a second story window and broke her back—and realized that her hard-partying lifestyle had to change. When an overweight, alcohol-addicted mom, Meredith Atwood, author of *Triathlon for the Every*

Woman, decided to conquer a triathlon, she points to the moment when a trainer told her she could.

Moments that lead us to finally say, enough is enough. Moments that motivate transformation. Real change comes only as the result of thousands of tiny steps taken toward a new future. But in every story of transformation, there is a moment when the person saw, with clarity and depth, that which was not working in her life. Often, but not always, that clarity comes at a moment of zero.

My hope for you is that you will be able to identify what's not working in your life, face it with absolute clarity, and begin the journey of transforming those things so you can have the life you truly want, and that you will be able to do so without hitting zero.

On our last walk, we talked about how lucky people keep their eyes up, both practically and metaphorically, to look for opportunities. Looking for the moments when your spirit is telling you what is not working can be very much the same. We all have an inner voice that wants to guide us to our best life. Often, that voice is buried beneath obligations and other people's expectations, but it is there. Inside of you. At this moment.

On today's walk, begin to tune in and learn to listen to that voice. *What is it telling you? What are the changes you need to make in your life?*

See if you can identify the most important shift you need to make in your life, and let's see if we can do it without hitting zero.

● ● ●

Walk # 15: The Problem with Oranges

I live on the east end of Long Island, two hours from New York City in a community with the ocean on one side and the Long Island Sound on the other. I love living here. I love the spring when the tourists and "weekend people" return and line the streets with BMWs and Teslas and the farm stands reopen their doors. I love the heart of summer when the ocean warms up and the farmers market opens each Sunday. And I love the fall after the tourists leave and the farm-stand tables are piled high with Brussels sprouts, late season lettuce, and the first local apples.

For six months of the year, our local produce is amazing. But when fall turns to winter, we are left with apples that have been around for a while, lettuce prepackaged in cellophane bags, and tomatoes that bear little resemblance to their summer counterparts. By February, I am desperate.

Florida's peak orange harvest season is February, exactly when the produce in New York is at its most meager. Last week, I picked up six gorgeous navel oranges while at the grocery store. And unlike more fragile fruits, like the mangos my kids love, oranges travel well. Bright and juicy, oranges are like sunshine in a fruit. I got home and placed them in a beautiful wooden bowl, right in the center of the kitchen table.

I love a good orange. I love how their light shade of orange brings a shot of color to the long grey days of the New York winter. I love the way the sections separate and fit perfectly in my mouth. And I love the smell of the orange peel on my hands after I have finished peeling it.

So why am I sitting at my kitchen table this morning, a *full week* later, staring at that bowl of oranges? Why haven't I eaten a *single* perfect orange in the past seven days?

Because oranges take too long to eat. Because I can't eat an orange while sitting at my computer answering emails, helping my kids with their homework, or driving to my next meeting. Because I can't eat an orange and multitask.

Oranges require my full attention to peel and to eat. I rarely give anything that is "not productive" or not on my to-do list my full attention. I drink my breakfast on the way to the office or the gym. I eat lunch at my computer. Nuts, popcorn, protein bars, and the occasional afternoon cookie or hunk of dark chocolate are all consumed one-handed in front of my computer.

Oranges are not so cooperative. They demand my full attention. I need two hands to peel them and while I'm eating them, my hands are juice-covered and cannot touch my keyboard. Don't think I haven't tried. If I peel one carefully and separate all of the sections, can I pop them in my mouth one by one while I work? The answer is no. Oranges require undivided attention.

The point? I realized this morning that I have created a life that is so jam-packed and focused on my to-do list that I don't have time to eat an orange in February.

That is crazy.

I suspect you have this same dilemma, and that in the busyness of your daily life there are simple pleasures that you have sacrificed. Instead, you chose to answer one more email before the kids stepped off the bus or the baby woke up from his nap. You passed up a moment to watch the sunset drop beneath the horizon. Two minutes to stretch a tight back. Three minutes to look up that recipe you've been wanting to try. Five minutes to play with the dog. Ten minutes to take a bath or call your best friend in New Orleans. Fifteen minutes to take a walk. Or the time it takes to peel and eat an orange.

On today's walk, think about the small things and simple pleasures that you don't step off the merry-go-round of your life and make time for. Then make a commitment to yourself to eat more oranges.

● ● ●

Walk # 16: 10 Habits of the Most Successful Moms

We often think of habits as negative things that we struggle to change: "bad habits." These include that afternoon cookie, diet soda, over-priced morning latte, yelling at your kids, or the granddaddy of all bad habits: smoking.

But habits are simply things we do reflexively, without stopping to think about them or figuring out how to do them. Because of that, habits don't require much brainpower. That makes good habits incredibly powerful for helping people simplify their day and cruise through them in the most productive way possible. For busy moms, the more we simplify our days, the better.

Through a collection of surveys and conversations, I've studied the most successful moms and have identified ten things they do as a matter of habit. But first, it is important to clarify what I mean by the "most successful moms." They are not moms whose kids are on the honor roll or moms who work full time, raise four kids, live in spotless homes, and volunteer sixteen hours each week. Instead, these are simply the moms who identify *themselves* as most successful. Moms who feel like they are on top of their game more often than not. Moms who wake up with enthusiasm for the day. Moms who, simply put, report a greater level of satisfaction and happiness with their lives.

Here's what those moms do.

1. **Go to Bed.** Most nights, they sleep at least seven hours.

2. **Get Up.** They get up before their kids. *Why*? It gives them a few minutes to transition from the quiet world of their dreams to the hectic world of their reality.

3. **Move**. While few moms exercise every day, those who are most successful make some form of physical activity part of their day at least three times each week. Yup, many of them walk regularly, either alone or with friends.

4. **Floss**. They floss. (Nope, I'm not kidding. Research says they floss.)

5. **Cubbies are King.** They have a designated place in their house—usually right by the door where their family comes in—where shoes, coats, boots, and backpacks are deposited. This reduces clutter and the instances of "mommy, I can't find my shoes" and helps provides a sense of control amidst the chaos.

6. **They Don't Go It Alone.** The most successful moms prioritize their relationships and spend between one and three hours with their friends each week, while moms who feel they are less successful report spending just an hour or less with friends.

7. **Real World First, Facebook Later.** While they are engaged on social media, they spend less time there than their less successful peers—averaging one to two hours daily as compared to three to four hours.

8. **Sup-Sup-Suppertime.** They sit down to dinner with their families an average of five times each week and mention communication with their kids as one of the keys to parenting success.

9. **My Name is... No**. Moms who feel more successful are far more likely to say no when asked to do something they really don't want to do, while moms who feel less successful are more likely to consider themselves "bad at saying no."

10. **Just Don't Look Under the Bed.** They keep their homes clean but not spotless, with the majority reporting "my house is pretty clean but just don't look under the beds" while less successful moms are more likely to report that "more often than not, there are dirty dishes in the sink, dust on the shelves and footprints on the floor."

I know, I know... you were looking for the magic bullet—the one thing you can do to transform the chaos that is motherhood. Sadly, the magic bullet doesn't exist. But if you identify two of these habits that are not currently part of your routine and incorporate them, you will begin to see a shift.

For today's walk, think about two positive habits, either from the list above or from your own life, that you would like to cultivate. Let's start small, with two little habits that you believe you could add to your daily routine.

Walk # 17: How to Cultivate Good Habits

Before I go to bed at night, I place the next day's gym clothes in a basket in the bathroom. The next morning, as I stumble into the bathroom at 5:00 AM, I reach for the clothes in the basket without a thought. By 5:05 AM, I am dressed for the gym.

That is my "cue."

We have a standing tradition of a work morning "huddle"—a group call during which the team briefly reviews its top priorities for the day. After the morning huddle, I grab my gym bag, hop in my car, and drive to the gym.

That is my routine.

I complete my workout and head back to my car feeling way, way better than I did when I arrived.

That is my reward. Going to the gym is a good habit that I execute on most days with very little thought.

Then, at 3:00 PM, I return home from the office and walk in the front door to wait for my kids to get off the bus.

That is my "cue."

I go directly to the kitchen and open the pantry where I pull out some nuts, chips, or cookies and sit back down at my computer for one last check of my email while I snack mindlessly and wait for the kids to come crashing through the door.

That is my routine.

I get to crunch on something salty or sweet in the few moments of afternoon peace.

That is my reward. Having something to munch on while I wait for the kids to get off the bus is a bad habit that I execute on most days and with very little thought.

Entire books have been written about habits. Developing new positive habits and changing old negative habits is not easy, even if you understand the formula. But understanding the basic mechanics of habits is a good place to start.

Boatloads of research, including an extensive study from MIT which is described in readable detail in *The Power of Habit* by Charles Duhigg have revealed two important things about habits.

First, habits have three distinct components: (1) the trigger or "cue," (2) the routine, and (3) the reward. Understanding this is awesome because it means that we can alter our habits—either encourage good ones or discourage bad ones—by changing these clearly defined elements.

Second, habits "light up" a different part of our brain than our more thoughtful actions and we execute them largely on autopilot. This is awesome because it means that once we ingrain a positive habit, we are far more likely to replicate it without having to "talk ourselves into it" every time. Because believe me, if I really stopped to think about all that is involved in going to the gym, I would rarely get in that car.

The bad news is that habits are very tricky things. New positive cues take time to cultivate while cues that trigger negative routines can't always be avoided. I will always walk into my house at about 3:00. Since habits primarily happen on autopilot, it takes a lot of mindfulness to alter them.

Creating a new habit is easier than obliterating an old one. So, one tactic that tends to work is to replace a "bad" habit with a "good" habit you'd like to foster. For instance, it will be easier to replace my afternoon snack with a new habit than it will be to simply do everything the same way—walk in the door, sit down at the computer, but don't get the snack.

Let's play with my afternoon snacking. I decided to try to replace my snacking habit with a ten-minute dog walk.

I began by hanging his leash on the door before I left for work—the new cue.

Settled on a ten-minute walk around the block—the routine.

Observed that after the walk, I felt refreshed, energized and had completely forgotten about the snack—the reward.

After a week, I discovered that not only have I begun to create a new habit for myself, I have created a habit for my dog: when I walk in the door after work (the cue) he expects a walk (the routine) and when we get home, he is happy (the reward). Apparently, dogs are habitual creatures as well.

On today's walk, think about one habit you identified on your last walk that you would like to begin to build. Don't overcomplicate it. Begin with something simple. It can be something from our last walk's list or something else. Consider what the cue is, what the routine is, and what the reward is. Then figure out how to change the cue and replace the routine.

Walk # 18: Fuel Up: Part 1

It's impossible to talk about big dreams without talking about the fuel it takes to provide the strength needed to do the work that it takes to get there. For many of us—dare I say for most of us—our relationship with food is kind of a mess. At the very least, it's probably complicated. It is tangled up with our self-image and caught up in our emotions and daily thoughts.

It's time we make peace with food.

I get it—I really do. I grew up in a world of athletes and dancers and figure skaters where weight was everything. Forty years later, in the most loving way possible, weight is one of the first subjects that comes up when I visit my parents. My dearest girlfriend once dove across a desk to knock a cookie out of my hand, and she did it out of love.

Over the past several years, I've thought about how great it would be to reclaim the hours of my life that I've spent thinking about, worrying about, or feeling bad about what I've eaten, the number on the scale, or the size of my ass. If a genie could restore all of those hours, I estimate I could add six years to my life.

But that time is gone, so let's just start with where we are today.

We are not our dress size, and our value is not defined by a number on a scale. Beautiful women, inside and out, come in all shapes, sizes, and colors. Society has done this horrible thing to women for decades: on the one hand, they have sold us an endless buffet of things that are delicious, but horrible for us, while on the other hand selling us a literally unattainable ideal of what we are supposed to look like. Then they topped that off with a raft of "diets" that promise impossible results, setting us up for failure after failure. It's no wonder we feel dispirited and discouraged.

The time has come for us to put an end to the food fight.

Food is a lot of things. It is fun, comfort, entertainment, and habit. But most of all, food is fuel. The only way you will be able to accomplish all you want to accomplish is if you fuel your body properly to produce the energy and power it needs.

It is that simple. For a moment, I'm asking you to put aside all of the issues and challenges you have with food and diet. Let go of the frustration with the failed diets, forget the comparison to magazine covers or your neighbor down the street. Just let it all go and think about food as fuel. Food as the magical substance that enables your body to produce milk for your babies, powers the creativity of your brain, and gives you the energy to get out of bed in the morning.

Let's look objectively at what food is and what it isn't. Food isn't your friend. Food can't fix loneliness or frustration. Food is fuel. That's it. Viewed through that lens, if you want the fuel that will enable you to accomplish all of the things you want to accomplish, then you need good, not crappy, fuel.

Twenty years ago, Eric and I committed what we called "the great puppy caper." We drove to Rhode Island to adopt our first dog from a breeder whose dogs were the smartest, kindest, funniest, and prettiest. We stood in her kitchen, getting final instructions on how to care for our new fur baby. These instructions ran two single-spaced pages long and, when she finished, she said, "Now the most important thing you have to do is to be sure he doesn't get overweight. You control his food, so make sure it is natural and healthy and don't let him eat too much." We looked at the breeder: all 250 pounds of her. "I know," she said. "I know how to keep my dogs fit and healthy, but not myself."

Sure you do, I thought. Make sure your food is natural and healthy and don't eat too much.

On today's walk, think about your relationship with food. I know what you're thinking: it's complicated, and that's okay. Just go ahead and let your mind ruminate on what food means to you. When you return, capture some of those thoughts. But make sure you end by writing down the words "Food is fuel."

Walk # 19: Fuel Up: Part 2

On our last walk, we explored our relationship with food. We dove into food habits and reminded ourselves that at the end of the day, food is fuel. Today, let's explore six food-related things that have enabled me to maintain a healthy weight, feel strong, fuel big workouts, and have the energy to chase big dreams. Of course, everyone's body is different and what works for me might not work for you. But these are the things that work for me.

1. Breakfast matters

I don't know if it is the "most important meal of the day" or not, but what I do know is that breakfast matters. Starting your day with crappy food, or no food at all, sets you up for a day of up and down energy, bad cravings, and poor choices. Breakfast needs some protein, some greens, and some whole grains. Oh, and as little sugar as possible.

We talked about my morning smoothie in Walk # 8 and here's the current version that I make pretty much every morning: no-sugar-added almond milk, vegan protein powder, kale, spinach, ginger, chia seeds, ground flax seeds, whatever fruit I have fresh or frozen (really, anything works: bananas, apples, strawberries, mango, blueberries), an eighth of an avocado (essential to make your smoothie, well, smooth and to give you the good fats you need to start your day) and three ice cubes.

Blend and done!

2.Sugar is bad

It just is. It causes your blood sugar to go up and down and does all kinds of bad things to your body. For many people, myself included, sugar triggers headaches, and for some, those headaches are migraines. The most insidious thing about sugar is that eating it makes you crave more of it. So, remember that handful of gummy bears you grabbed at 11:00 AM? It isn't just those five gummy bears. It is five gummy bears that are going to make it really, really hard for you to resist another five gummy bears at 2:00 PM.

Sugar has consequences.

3.Soda is worse

Soda is like mainlining sugar. It is like shooting sugar into your veins the way a junkie shoots heroin. There is not one single reason to drink soda. No, you don't need the caffeine. No, you don't need the sugar boost.

Because we know that the small things matter, here's a little math. A can of soda has 140 calories, which, standing on its own, doesn't sound like that many. Putting aside the fact that mainlining 39 grams of sugar will cause your insulin to spike and set you up for a day of up and down energy and make you crave more sugar...if you drink just one can of soda a day, that is 51,100 calories a year, which will equate to about a fifteen-pound weight gain. Now, I believe that counting calories is *not* the best way to go about things and I'm not suggesting you count the calories of everything you eat. However, when you do the math of what a single can of soda each day does, well, just drink water.

4.No good comes from eating at night

When Eric and I first moved from the city to the country, we didn't put a TV in our bedroom. "Bedrooms are for sleeping and sex," the experts said. So instead, the TV was in the living room, which was right next to the kitchen. I vividly recall watching *The Amazing Race* while eating cereal straight from the box. After three years, I realized how much I missed laying in my bed and watching television. I know, I know, watching TV is a waste of time, but at the end of a long day, the forty minutes I spend lost in someone else's drama from the comfort of my bed is heaven. Anyway, the moral of the story is that once we moved the TV to the bedroom, I immediately lost four pounds.

No good comes from eating late night snacks. Have a nutritious, satisfying dinner. Finish dinner. Do dishes. Then call the kitchen closed.

5.Eat more vegetables

Okay, here's the truth. Until you do it and do it for a while, asparagus will not taste as good as Oreos. But one is fuel, and one is poison. It is estimated that there are 20,000 types of edible plants in the world and there are hundreds of different ways to prepare them: you can steam them, roast them, mash them, grill them, blend them into smoothies, add them to a stew, combine them into a salad or eat them raw. Just to name a few.

Eat them. Every meal, every day. Just eat more vegetables.

6.Drink More Water

You don't *need* soda, juice, or wine. You might think you do, but you don't. What you *need* is water and probably more of it than you are getting now. While there are differing opinions on exactly how much water you need, research shows that even mild dehydration can dampen your mood, reduce your ability to concentrate, increase the likelihood of headaches and drain your energy—and without those things function-ing at their best, there is no way you can do the work you need to do to crush your dreams.

Chances are, you need more water. Drink it.

Okay, those are six things I know for sure about myself and food. On today's walk, think about the things you know for sure about food. Be honest, remember, no one is watching.

Walk # 20: Fifteen Seconds

My first job out of law school was with a huge national law firm. I was a litigator and spent most of my time representing large businesses locked in battle with other businesses, executives or, sometimes, the government. I was twenty-three years old and loved my gorgeous suits, riding the elevator to the 42nd floor each morning, hearing about the weekend escapades of our receptionist on Monday mornings, and the huge bouquet of fresh flowers that brightened the office. Generally, I found the people great and the work challenging. It was a good place to launch my career.

One Saturday morning, on a perfect June day, all of the first-year associates were required to attend a full-day accounting workshop to learn the fundamentals of public accounting. This was important because much of our work involved business disputes. We needed to understand the boxes of financial documents at the heart of these lawsuits.

I hate accounting. Balance sheets simultaneously bore me and make my head spin. An 8:00 AM accounting class had resulted in the poorest grade of my entire college career. Clearly, this Saturday workshop was one that I would have benefited from.

After a long and tedious morning, we broke for lunch. I walked outside where the weather was glorious. It was a perfect spring day with a bright blue sky and hint of a breeze. I sat down on a bench and ate a sandwich, then stopped at The Gap to buy a new white t-shirt before heading back upstairs to the windowless conference room where the workshop was being held. The two CPAs began to talk, again, about balance sheets and the difference between compiled, reviewed, and audited financial statements. Above their heads was a large clock. I watched fifteen seconds tick by.

And I thought, *I have no idea how long my life will be, but I just lost fifteen seconds of it that I can't get back*. I couldn't sit there another moment.

"I'm leaving," I whispered to my friend Marina, who was sitting next to me.

"You can't leave," she whispered back.

"Yeah," I said, "I can."

I packed up my notebook, grabbed the bag that held my new white t-shirt and walked out into the sunshine. The firm wasn't happy with me, but they didn't fire me and, somehow, I managed to have a successful legal career without spending that afternoon in that conference room.

My mother-in-law was recently diagnosed with Type 2 diabetes and was forced to take a good, hard look at what she was eating. "I had no idea," she told me on a recent visit. "Every time I walked into the house I would grab a little something. I never sat down and ate a pint of ice cream, but it was the little things, a cookie here, a bite of chocolate there."

Guess what. Your very valuable time is being eaten in just the same way. Ten minutes on Facebook here, five minutes looking for stray socks there.

The seconds of your life come in a limited supply and they tick away one by one. Once spent, you do not get them back. Do not squander those precious seconds. Yes, there are things that we have to do. Things we do for our families. Things we do for our friends. Things we do for society. Things we do for our dogs. Even things we do for ourselves that align with our larger goals. I hate washing and cutting up vegetables, but I like healthy eating. I hate making my bed, but I love coming home to a tidy, inviting home. I hate answering emails, but I love connecting with my colleagues.

Before you head out on today's walk, I want you to look at your clock, watch, or phone and watch one entire minute go by. Go ahead, I'll wait.

Okay, your life is now one minute shorter. I have no idea how much time you have on this earth to walk in the sunshine, hold hands with someone you love, or watch your children grow, but I do know that your available bucket is now sixty seconds shorter.

If you come to your life with genuine mindfulness about what is important to you, if you regularly ask yourself "what matters" in the long term, if you stop spending those precious moments doing things that you don't want to, and don't have to do, you can infuse your life with more joy, more meaning, and more fun.

On today's walk, identify three things you do that: 1) don't bring you joy and 2) don't align with your larger goals. Then make a decision to stop doing at least one of them.

● ● ●

Walk # 21: Vampires and Demons

Years ago, I read a novel about vampires and demons. Demons, as portrayed in this novel, are beings who feed on drama and intrigue. They thrive on the suffering of others. The smart demons chose professions that gave them a steady diet of the worst of humankind and delivered a constant stream of drama and upset. They were homicide detectives, emergency room doctors, and crime reporters. They did pretty well adapting to and moving through life because their need for drama was regularly satiated. But the other demons felt compelled to create unrest and upheaval. They were constantly stirring up trouble because they needed it to feel good. In short, they were addicted to drama.

The vampires required the lifeblood of others in order to survive. While some controlled their appetite sufficiently by taking just a sip here and a sip there, others, well, once they got started, they sucked their victims dry.

Though I don't recall much else about the book, these two character types stayed with me because I realized that, although they might not be supernatural creatures like those portrayed in the novel, demons and vampires live amongst us.

For a long time, I believed that drama just followed some people. We all know people who always seem to be embroiled in one drama or another. For sure, some of that is bad luck or unfortunate events. But I've come to realize that some people crave drama and, much like the demons in the book, will create it if necessary. Often unconsciously, but nevertheless, they make choices in their lives that foster drama. They move from one crisis to another. You can recognize these people by the litany of dramatic events in their lives, the way their eyes light up at the telling of those tales, or the way that they seem to get antsy when things are just a bit too calm. The way they self-sabotage their success is astonishing.

Now, at the same time, demons can be lots of fun. They are constantly in motion. Oftentimes they are smart and funny and have really good stories to tell. But be careful, because these are the people who feed on drama—anyone's drama. If you are going to be in their whirlwind, then you run the risk of getting caught up in their drama.

Then there are the bloodsuckers—the vampires. Those are the people who manage to suck the joy and energy from you. They do this in a variety of ways, and that sometimes makes them more difficult to identify. The partner or parent or sibling who belittles you in small and subtle ways. The friend who talks entirely about themselves, leaving no room for you. Basically, anyone who leaves you feeling depleted—mentally or physically—after you've spent time together.

Chances are that demons and vampires will move in and out of your life. They could be a neighbor. A sister. Maybe your mother or your mother-in-law. Friends who complain nonstop about their husbands, jobs, or children, or others who are constantly gossiping about others. Recognizing vampires is tricky because you have to tune in to how you feel after spending time with them. We all have people in our lives who, after we spend time with them, leave us feeling energized, lighter, or happier. Conversely, after spending time with a vampire, you're left feeling tired, sapped, or saddened.

How you manage demons and vampires depends on where they fit into your life. It would be easy to say "just don't let these people in," but the truth is, there are people who are going to be in your life no matter what. It comes down to relationship management, and managing your relationships with demons and vampires requires three things.

First, you must recognize them for who they are and remember that they will not change. Your mother will not stop criticizing you, your sister-in-law will never step out of the whirlwind of drama she has created, and the mother of your daughter's best friend will never stop gossiping about the rest of the third-grade parents. This is who they are. They will not change. See them with clarity and realize that their need to create drama or desire to feed on your energy is not about you, it is about them. Whatever you do, don't bother trying to change them because that will do nothing but exhaust you.

Second, decide if you can continue to invite these people into your world, or if you can limit your exposure to them. Remember, a vampire can only enter your house if invited. You decide where these creatures fit, and you control how much time you spend with them or how much power and influence they have.

Finally, remember that this is about them and not you. Your mother is not criticizing you because of you, she is criticizing you because of how it makes her feel. That other mom is not gossiping because of you, she is gossiping because of how it makes her feel. The friend who constantly needs to be bailed out of the drama she creates? Yup, that's about her, not you.

Sometimes, we can simply choose not to let demons and vampires into our lives. But sometimes we either can't limit our exposure to them, or we choose not to. In those instances, recognize them for who and what they are and erect walls to keep them from exerting their negative influence. Remembering that their issues are about them—and not us—can help us navigate these relationships without being sucked into the vortex of the demons' drama or sacrificing our lifeblood to the vampires.

On today's walk, think about the vampires and demons in your life. Who are they and how do they impact you?

Walk # 22: Your Three People

A million years ago, Eric and I were launching our first business. We had quit our New York City jobs, sold our apartment, moved to the Hamptons, adopted the dog-of-all-dogs who we named Kibo, and launched the Rover Group, a company that manufactured dog treats, horse treats, and cat treats.

We were at our first trade show and our booth was set up. With about thirty minutes left before the show doors opened, Eric went off to walk a few aisles and check out the other booths. He returned and said, "I found you a friend." I followed his directions to a booth that sold high-end dog clothes and collars run by a lady named Sue. Sue vibrated with positive energy, and I knew within moments that we would be friends for life.

When I was two years old, my grandmother lived in the same house in which she had raised my mother and her three siblings in a small neighborhood called Kensington. We would go visit often, and for a rambunctious two-year-old, there was little to do. But just next door lived Bea, who was visited often by her daughter and granddaughter, Lorelei. When the stars aligned, Lore and I were there on the same day and I can recall, even now, playing in the backyard of my grandmother's house in stretchy Danskin shorts and tops. We have now been friends for fifty years. Fifty years.

When I was in High School, I had the good fortune to be part of a posse. I was the only girl among five boys and, wow, did we have fun together. Michael was often the instigator, the one who pushed us to get together and have adventures. The one who dragged me, kicking and screaming, onto Lightning Loops at Great Adventure. The one who swore we would all be friends for life. When we grew up, he married a wonderful woman who also became a dear friend. Then we all had kids around the same age and our kids began to grow up together. But, then we got busy. Too busy.

Sue lives in New Jersey. Michael and his wife live in New Jersey. Lorelei lives in New Orleans. I have two kids, two dogs, and a business to raise. That is a formula that doesn't allow for a whole lot of time with the people you love. That is a formula that makes it easy to let days and then weeks and then months and then years go by. That is a formula that makes relationships, even with people you care deeply about, very difficult to maintain.

Often that's okay. Not every friend is destined to be a friend for life. It is okay for friends, even good friends, to come and go in your life. It is okay to have friends for specific seasons of your life. But, if you are lucky, deliberate, thoughtful, and mindful, there will be a small handful of friends with whom you share a deep bond that transcends time and distance and life stages. These are the people who you will see, even after a long absence, and you will feel like no time has passed. You will find yourself saying things like, "We pick up right where we left off."

But.

All relationships must be nurtured and cared for and attended to. All relationships take work and effort. If you have these people in your life, these friends for life, consider yourself deeply blessed and then be sure you are consciously making the effort to maintain those relationships. This takes work and effort, but probably less than you think.

Consider what I call "the pyramid of connection." At the bottom of the pyramid is staying connected via social media. This is one of those positive uses of social media—the chance to keep up, in a very cursory way, with what is going on in their lives. Rather than getting sucked mindlessly into the morass of memes, use your social media time deliberately to stay connected with the people who are important to you.

In the middle of the pyramid is time spent talking to each other by phone. If you both are busy, like really busy, this time is often better scheduled. Lorelei and I will often actually schedule calls and put them on the calendar as we would any other important appointment.

At the top of the pyramid is time together. In person. This is, of course, the most difficult to manage with friends who live apart, especially when you each have kids and work and homes and pets. But it is essential to maintaining deep and meaningful relationships that you find a way to be together, in person, to have those long meandering conversations that are the bedrock of friendship.

I have failed at this with my dear friend Sue. We are both so busy and, though she lives only three hours away, I haven't seen her in person in nearly a decade. I feel I have failed her as a friend. Today, I will reach out and make a plan to see her one way or the other.

On today's walk, think about those people in your life, especially the long-distance friends, who mean the world to you. Then make a commitment to doing the work to keep those connections.

Walk # 23: Decision Fatigue

My sister is a designer for one of the top jewelers in the world. Her office is flanked by hundreds of drawers holding tens-of-thousands of semi-precious stones in every imaginable shade, shape, and size. Each day, she is charged with combining those stones into dozens of beautiful creations. Each day, she leaves work exhausted.

"You don't understand," she says. "At the end of the day, I have absolutely nothing left. No energy. Nothing."

But wait. She works in a nice office, surrounded by beautiful jewelry, and spends most of her day sitting at a desk. There is no physical labor and all the coffee she can drink. *Why is she so tired by the end of the day?*

It's called decision fatigue and it is a real thing. Not only does it exhaust you, but it causes you to make increasingly poor decisions with each additional decision you are forced to make.

Decision fatigue is the reason why stores place candy at the checkout counter—they know that you have used up much of your good-decision making energy choosing between the twenty-six different types of peanut butter offered in aisle five. It is the reason that by 4:00 PM, deciding what to make for dinner can be downright debilitating.

My personal decision fatigue is largely the result of the 400-plus emails that land in my inbox every day. While they don't all require a thoughtful response, every one of them requires a decision about how they should be handled. It's exhausting and has led me on a quest to better understand decision fatigue and to develop strategies to combat it. While there is no one magic cure, here are five strategies that can help.

First, understand that decision fatigue is real. Appreciate that you will only be able to make a limited number of good decisions each day. Learn to be judicious in how you spend your high-quality decision-making capital.

Second, do whatever you can to limit the number of decisions you have to make. Then, make the most important decisions early in the day. President Obama and Mark Zuckerberg wear the same thing every day for the express purpose of removing one decision from their morning. I create a lunch "checklist" for my kids so that they can select what they want in their lunchbox based on what we shopped for on Sunday. Indulgent? Nope. It means they are more likely to eat what is in their lunch and, more importantly, I don't have to decide what to pack them.

Third, accept the fact that no decision is perfect, and each will be a balance of pros and cons. The all-natural peanut butter is more expensive, the reduced fat has additives, and your kids prefer regular. Unless peanut butter is very important to you for some reason, choose one and move on.

Fourth, don't second guess a decision once made. Some decisions will work out and others won't and no amount of second-guessing will prevent you from making mistakes. In fact, the only thing second-guessing a decision will do is burn more of your precious decision-making capacity, which is better spent on the next decision.

Finally, recognize that it is impossible to know which decisions will ultimately be the most important. Years ago, I was wrestling with an important life decision and, as is my way, I needed to talk it to death. I flew to Florida and spent the weekend wearing out my very patient parents with an endless loop of pros and cons, *should I* and *shouldn't I*'s.

Finally my mother said, "You just have to make a decision."

"But you don't understand," I whined. "This is the most important decision of my life."

Her reply? "No. You don't know what the most important decision of your life will be. It could be turning right instead of left when you leave your building in the morning: if you turn right you could get hit by a taxi and if you turn left, you could meet the great love of your life."

Yes, our lives are the product of the decisions we make. Yes, we strive to make good decisions. But your life will be the result of far-reaching implications of decisions that you can't possibly fathom. All we can do is hold tight to our decision-making capabilities, be mindful of managing the inevitable decision fatigue, and soldier on.

On today's walk, consider that every single decision you make depletes your capacity, and contemplate where in your typical day you are expending unnecessary decision-making energy. Could you make a meal plan and avoid the "what's for dinner" decision? Automate delivery of some key things you purchase like toilet paper and dish detergent? Commit to a daily "uniform"?

Let's get precious with our decision-making capacity and reserve as much as possible for the things that matter most.

● ● ●

Walk # 24: Tomorrow Starts Today

By the time I crawl into my bed at about 8:30 (or sometimes before then), I am done in. I have nothing left. Depleted, deployed, and empty. I give myself over to that feeling and will sometimes flip through a magazine or watch an episode of mindless TV.

My days are long. I am up early. Like 5:00 AM early. Getting two kids off to school, working, hitting the gym, working some more. Walking, thinking, and writing. Making dinner. Doing laundry. Walking the dog. 400 emails. And a big dose of the decision fatigue we talked about on our last walk.

Trust me, I know tired.

But before I crawl into bed, I do five things, each one specifically designed to focus my mind, improve my health, and set myself up for success for the coming day. Here are my five things.

Coffee

I set up the coffee pot. I'm usually up by 5:00, when the house is still and quiet. I covet my early mornings as they are the most productive time of my day. I protect them fiercely (more on mornings another day). But I confess that it is sometimes the promise of a hot cup of coffee that is *the thing* that launches me out of a warm bed and into a cold house. I wish I was a person who could start her day with a cup of warm water with lemon. Or apple cider vinegar. Or herbal tea. But I'm not. It's a big mug of steaming black coffee for me.

Whatever your favorite morning beverage, it should be ready and waiting. When you finish the dinner dishes, take an extra 30 seconds to put whatever you need right on your kitchen counter. Your favorite mug and the fixings of your favorite morning beverage.

Tidy My Bedroom

Okay, so this is the one I hate the most because I hate sorting laundry. And somehow, it seems there is often a load of washed but unfolded laundry sitting on my bed when I head upstairs for the night. Or the clothes I took off after work are laying on the chair in the bedroom. Or a pile of unread papers is sitting on my nightstand beside yesterday's glass of water.

Whatever it is, take a few minutes to tidy up your bedroom. Not a major clean up—don't get sucked down the rabbit hole and decide that 10:00 PM is the perfect time to sort your sock drawer. Just five to ten minutes to tidy it up.

Lay Out the Morning Clothes

I start most days in workout clothes and I always, always pull them out of the closet and put them in a basket in the bathroom before I go to bed. This way I'm dressed and ready before I have the chance to think about whether or not I really want to go to the gym or head out for an early walk. Perhaps more importantly, it removes one decision from my morning, reducing the onset of the decision fatigue we talked about on our last walk.

Floss

I hate flossing. It is time-consuming and annoying. Some nights, it makes my gums bleed and that is, well, kinda gross. I also have a very small mouth, so getting to those back teeth isn't easy.

But I do it anyway. Every night.

Why? Because I hate going to the dentist and if there's anything I can do to minimize the time spent in the dentist's chair, I'm in. Second, I believe it helps with bad breath. Third, there is evidence that people with poor oral health have higher rates of cardiovascular problems (including heart attacks and strokes). Finally, as we talked about in Walk 16, the happiest and most successful moms floss, so there must be something to it.

Practice Gratitude

There is no better time to contemplate all you have to be grateful for than right before bed. It provides the chance to appreciate all that is good. This practice is about taking a moment to reflect on your day, express gratitude, and think about people you love.

Take a moment before bed to make a quick entry in the gratitude journal that sits on the night-table beside your bed. *Wait, you don't have one?* Okay, go get a small notebook, a pen that writes well (perhaps in a favorite color), and put them beside your bed. Each night before you go to sleep, capture one thing for which you are grateful. Don't overthink it. My entries have included everything from gratitude for the support of my parents as I was growing up, to the health of my children, to the hot coffee that will be awaiting me in the morning. There are no rules.

Define Tomorrow's Priorities

The power of the mind while sleeping shouldn't be underestimated. So, you might as well put it to work for you. The easiest way to do this is to grab your goalpost notebook. *Wait, you don't have one of those either?* Okay, get yourself a notebook or a scrap of paper—really anything will work to get started. Write down your goals for the month on the front page (in really big letters). Then, each night, before you go to bed, write down the three most important things you need to accomplish the next day.

Now, sometimes what you need to "accomplish" the most is more of an intention than an action. For instance, if what you need most is a day of rest and recuperation, set an intention to have a "no rules day"—a concept we'll talk about later. If you have a family day planned, set your intention to be as present as possible.

On today's walk, think about your evening routine. What are your pre-bedtime habits? Are you lying in bed scrolling social media and feeling FOMO from a friend's recent vacation or anger from a recent political debate? Are you still up doing that last bit of laundry? Do you finally fall into bed, face unwashed and teeth unbrushed?

Where are the areas for improvement? What evening routine could you create that would enable you to mindfully close the chapter on the day and set yourself up for a fantastic day to come?

When you get back from today's walk, write down three to five specific tasks you will do each night. Post them where you will see them, perhaps on your bathroom mirror. For one month, commit to doing each of these things every single night. Yes. Every. Single. Night. At the end of the month, see if they've resulted in a shift in how you launch the next day, how productive you are, and, most importantly, how happy you are.

Walk # 25: Go To Sleep

Oh, the irony. At 2:18 AM, I was wide awake staring at the ceiling. On my mind? *What to write about this morning.* Then it hit me: the importance of sleep.

Now, I love sleep. I fact, I love few things as much as I love crawling into bed at the end of a busy day and falling into slumber. I know, without any doubt, that I perform better, am more productive, more patient, and happier when I consistently book seven to eight hours of sleep. A good night's sleep recharges my brain, body, and spirit. Since I'm up at 5:00 AM, that means I go to bed by 9:00 PM. During the month of June, that means I sometimes go to sleep before the sun has fully set.

Sleep is awesome. According to research from the National Sleep Foundation, adults between the ages of 26 and 64 need seven to ten hours of sleep each night. Okay, that's not groundbreaking, but compared to the average night's sleep for most people, it is clear people are simply not sleeping long enough.

It amazes me how few women sleep enough hours. In our State of Mom survey, we discovered that *less than* 30% of moms average at least seven hours of sleep each night, while a full 25% don't even sleep six.

Who cares? We get up every day and do what needs to be done. We survive the days and somehow our kids are still alive and there is still a roof over our heads. We soldier on, exhausted perhaps, but we keep moving forward.

So, is getting enough sleep really that important?

Yup. Sure is.

Shorting yourself of even one hour of the sleep your body needs can make you drowsy, lethargic, and less likely to effectively take care of yourself. This includes essential daily aspects—like exercise and walking. Lack of quality sleep impacts your ability to make good decisions—like deciding to eat that second piece of chocolate cake. It can increase your irritability, make you short-tempered, and more likely to yell at your kids or snap at your partner. It impairs driving abilities and increases the odds of an accident. It diminishes creativity and dampens your ability to experience joy. It impedes your ability to process and remember. It makes your body prone to weight gain.

It negatively impacts immune systems, increasing your odds of catching a cold or flu. Even worse, lack of sleep increases your risk of heart disease, stroke, cancer, and possibly dementia.

Seriously, all of this can be the result of only six hours of sleep instead of seven-and-a-half hours of sleep. All of this.

Now I know you might believe that you function just fine on six hours of sleep. After all, you are getting it all done. But I am telling you, with absolute certainty, that you are not getting it done as well as you could be. Perhaps more importantly, you are not feeling as vital, energetic, or happy as you could be.

It is a simple equation: less sleep equals less capacity for joy. Okay, so how? How do you get more sleep?

For many of us, the answer is simple: you must prioritize sleep. That means prioritizing it over that last load of laundry. Prioritizing it over social media. Prioritizing it over making home-baked cookies for little Timmy's second grade Halloween party. At times, you might even have to prioritize it over work. We must rebuild our habits to make sleep something we cherish, covet, and love.

For others, simply prioritizing sleep might not be enough and professional help might be needed. If this is you—if you've read the articles, turned off the screens, drank the chamomile tea, darkened the room, learned to meditate—and it still isn't helping, please know that you are not alone.

According to the American Sleep Association, between 50 and 70 million Americans have chronic sleep disorders. Poor sleep is practically an epidemic and, as of 2013, the American Academy of Sleep Medicine had accredited 2,500 sleep centers across the US. If you need the help, go get the help.

A final thought. If you have a new baby in the house or, for that matter, a new puppy, all bets are off. Know that you can survive short-term sleep deprivation. You will not be at your best, but you will survive the coming months of sleepless nights. But once that baby—or puppy—starts sleeping through the night, you must too.

As you walk today, think about how you relate to sleep. Do you treat it like the priority it should be? If not, what needs to change to enable you to do that? Do you need a mindset change? Change of habits? Or do you need professional help? Make a commitment to making whatever changes you must to get the sleep you need.

● ● ●

Walk # 26: Failure Sucks... and is Awesome

**"Success is stumbling from failure to failure
with no loss of enthusiasm."**
— Winston Churchill

Macaroni Kid, the company I founded and helped build, was doing great. We were growing every year and staying true to our core mission: empowering more than 500 local moms to build hyper-local media empires in their own communities and sharing content each and every week that genuinely made families' lives better. Our advertisers, who were the clients who kept the lights on and the engine going, were happy.

Things were good. But they weren't good enough. We had 500 local affiliates, but there were millions more moms. Many of those women had taken a step away from their careers when they had kids, but they still had energy and creativity and wanted to help provide for their families. And my mission, which I scribbled in the notebook where I write down my dreams and my goals, answered the question "who do I want to be" in this way:

A leader of women, who seeks to make the world a better place by inspiring them <u>and</u> by giving them the tools to become their best selves.

Giving tools to 500 women and fostering a community of support was awesome. But it wasn't enough. I was ready to try something new.

Coffee. Lots of women drink coffee. We would create a company that empowered women to sell quality coffee on a subscription basis. That makes sense: women drink a lot of coffee and a subscription means you don't have to go to the store to get it, which lets your customers cross one thing off their list.

We sourced the BEST coffee. Truly. We created an amazing brand identity.

And we failed. Hard.

Next? Accessories. We stumbled upon a factory that made handbags and backpacks out of gorgeous, supple rubber (I promise, they were much cooler than they sound). But in the sourcing process, we got pulled off course and released a line of shoes and bracelets. Shoes and bracelets? What were we thinking? Failure number two.

And there were others. So many projects we tried that didn't work as planned. Macaroni TV, Macaroni Tribes, Macaroni Live. We bought a small company that failed. We hosted events that no one came to. The list goes on.

Last year, we moved our offices from the place we had been in for more than a decade, a space that was bright and open and had a 2,000 square foot basement that we had filled. In order to move, we needed to purge that entire basement. It was full of our failed projects. I remember standing at the door of the basement, looking at everything that had to be sorted, given away, sold, or tossed. In one corner, boxes of documents from legal cases I had worked on more than a decade before. In the middle of the floor, boxes of shoes and bracelets from our failed accessories company. Against the far wall, cases of packaging from our failed coffee company. In a back corner, the green screen and lights for the "studio" we had set up to record the videos for Macaroni TV. And in the right-hand corner, everything one would need to put on an incredible live event... that no one would come to.

Cleaning that basement was devastating. It was a two-week journey picking through all of my failed projects and bad ideas.

Failure sucks.

But.

The only way you will discover what works is by trying it. It is impossible to know with certainty that something is going to be successful until you do the work and bring it to life. You will only grow and learn if you are willing to try things that you haven't tried before. If you push outside your comfort zone and take risks.

There are three things that make it possible to go from failure to failure without loss of enthusiasm.

First, you must understand that just because a project failed, you are not a failure. You tried something that didn't work. But you cannot let failure define you. That project failed, but you are not a failure. Words are important, so say, "That didn't work out as planned," and never say, "I am a failure." Life is long. There will be other opportunities.

Second, you must remember that just because something you tried failed doesn't mean that the next thing you try will fail. We learn and grow every day. Every failure and setback teaches us lessons that make us stronger and wiser. The next thing might fail, but it might not. Then there's the thing after that.

And that leads to number three: you must learn from your failures. Sometimes that takes some time. You might need a little distance from the failure to give yourself the objectivity needed to identify the causes of the failure. It is easy to close the door on projects that didn't work. Examining them is painful. Trust me, I know. But examining them is essential. Where were your faulty assumptions? Did you ignore your gut, do too little research, or quit too soon?

On today's walk, think about one or two times you have failed. I know, who wants to revisit those times? But trust me, as long as enough time has passed, it will be okay. Dig in and think about why those things failed and identify two lessons you can learn from each experience.

● ● ●

Walk # 27: More Musings from the Bathroom Floor

I'm sitting on the bathroom floor of a hotel room in Jamaica. It is day one of a four-day mother-daughter vacation, just me and my daughter, who is thirteen. Just the two of us. I suspect that some of you who are—or have been—a mother to a young teen, just let out a heavy sigh on my behalf.

But this isn't about mother-daughter relationships, about which I am no expert. Rather, it is about finding ways to change the patterns of behavior that we fall into, especially with those who are closest to us. Patterns I am determined to break, at least for these four days.

Here's what those patterns often look like with my daughter and me. I do something that "annoys" her, which can be, well, anything, because she's a teenage girl and I'm her mother. So, by definition, I'm annoying at least 60% of the time. She cops "that attitude" or answers with "that tone." I get angry and, though I rarely lose my temper, I "explain" to her why her attitude is unacceptable. I'm left with a bitter taste in my mouth and, presumably, so is she.

These kinds of patterns reveal themselves in other relationships as well. Eric forgets to do something he promised to do and I get the familiar feeling that I am not a priority. My mother says something critical; I snap back, feeling simultaneously hurt and angry—*I'm a grown-ass woman with limited resources, so no thank you, I can't buy a new couch even though the one I have is showing its age.*

Those patterns even arise in my own head, in my own voice whenever the business has a bad month, I gain a few pounds, I miss a few workouts, or I go for that second piece of chocolate cake. Or anytime I start a project that I don't finish. Whenever I don't lead the team the way I should. Whatever it is, whenever I feel that I've come up short, the following words run through my head: *you suck.*

Our patterns and our habits not only come to define us, but they are not easy to change. However, it *is* possible to change them.

How?

Step One: Recognize, really recognize, the patterns we have in our relationships with others and with ourselves. Strive to see them for what they are and how they play out. Do you have the same conversations over and over? Feel the same feelings? It often helps to try to write them down, though I know that can feel like torture.

Step Two: Have a very genuine desire to change these repeating situations, which starts by letting go of the need to be right. So often, especially in disagreements with those closest to us, we have a need to be right. Frankly, I'm not sure why. I have the need for my daughter to acknowledge that she's speaking to me in a snotty, teenage way, the need for my mother to acknowledge that I'm a grown-ass woman, and the need for Eric to reaffirm that I am a priority.

Step Three: Take your awareness of those patterns and change them. The best way to start this type of change is to be on the lookout for moments when you head down those familiar paths. Instead, stop yourself and consciously choose a different response.

So, this week, while in Jamaica, I promised myself to try to shift the dynamic. Here's my plan. When I do something "annoying" and she gives me "that look" or "that tone," I'm going to calmly say, "I understand you're frustrated that I won't stay up to go with you to the midnight glow party, but that's just too late for me and for you." Then I'm going to let it go. I won't recite all of the awesome things we did during the course of the day, or try to make her acknowledge that her request was ridiculous. Most of all, I will try not to allow the feelings of hurt and anger in the pit of my stomach that indicate that somehow I am not doing a good enough job as her mother because if I were, she wouldn't be such a... teen.

On today's walk, think about one pattern you find yourself in with those who are closest to you, and identify just how to work toward shifting it. Over time, add another pattern and another pattern.

Walk # 28: Pearl's Basement (or) What's the Worst that Could Happen?

It was 1998 and Eric and I had just gotten married. We had good jobs—great jobs, really. I was a litigator at the premiere entertainment litigation firm in New York City and spent my days fighting the battles of people like Julie Andrews and Jon Bon Jovi. I rode in a limousine with Santana and spent a year with the family of Jonathan Larson—the genius who created the hit Broadway show *RENT*. I wore beautiful suits and made enough money to support myself and buy a small "weekend" house in the Hamptons. It was a very small house, just two bedrooms, but it was on a lovely piece of property and sat just two miles from the ocean. We loved it. Eric was working as the marketing director for a publicly-traded entertainment company. We almost didn't get past our second date, as he interrupted it three times to negotiate a deal in Australia. He was traveling, challenged, and had tremendous opportunities in front of him.

We were living a big life. But it wasn't *our* life. We'd spend Sunday nights talking about all of the things we could do that would enable us to quit our jobs, sell our apartment, and move to the Hamptons fulltime.

One day we had an idea. We'd been watching the start of the nutrition bar revolution—at the time there were only a few on the market, but they were gaining traction—and we thought, *okay, what if we create a snack bar for dogs? Dogs get hungry, right?* If you take your dog hiking or to the beach for the entire day, they probably need a snack just like you do. We did some research and found that yup, just like people, dogs burn calories and, when they are very active, could use a snack. The idea for the Rover Bar was born and with it began the endless loop of conversation that we called the "go or no go decision": should we quit our jobs, sell our apartment, and start a business? We would walk through what that would look like. Though we knew nothing about financial projections or business plans, we'd try to create them. Yet, at the end of each conversation, we asked the same question: *what if we fail?*

Honestly, we were very, very afraid to fail.

Now, sometimes fear is good, because sometimes it keeps us from doing really, really stupid things. But sometimes fear keeps us from doing really, really awesome things too.

Beyond being afraid to quit my safe, secure, and very lucrative job as a lawyer in order to move to the beach and start a business, I was afraid to have a baby (I can't even begin to list my becoming-a-mom fears). I was afraid to host my first webinar (so I canceled, twice). And I was terrified at the prospect of putting this book out into the world (what if you hate it?).

Being a bit of a rebel, I will often take action in spite of fear, but it's not easy. Like a lot of people, I have a constant voice in my head warning me to "be careful" and "don't risk too much." Big dreams and big chances present big risks. Change presents risk. Risk creates fear. Change creates fear.

So, the question is: *how do you manage the fear?*

The answer is—Pearl's basement.

Pearl is Eric's mother and she lives in a nice townhouse about an hour north of New York City. Her townhouse has a finished basement with a small bedroom and a tiny bathroom.

"If we lose everything," Eric said, "we can always live in Pearl's basement."

And there it was—the worst-case scenario. We wouldn't be homeless. We'd be embarrassed. We'd be scared. We'd be broke. But, if all else failed, at least we wouldn't be homeless.

So, we took the leap. We quit our jobs, sold our apartment, moved to our tiny house and started The Rover Group. Three years later, we had lost almost everything. We hadn't moved into Pearl's basement yet, but we had borrowed money from friends and family and still, the losses kept piling up. And then our bags broke.

We had doubled-down and committed to all new packaging, which we had manufactured in China. I remember the day the new packaging arrived on the front lawn. We opened the boxes and the packaging was gorgeous. This was exactly what we needed to take our business to the next level. The very next day, we loaded it all up and off we went to introduce it at the biggest trade show of the year. We had one day to set up our booth, and as we hung the bags—now filled with treats—on display racks, one by one the bottoms fell out and the treats crashed to the floor.

Without telling us, the manufacturer had decided to use a different material that he thought would look better, but the seals didn't hold. In a panic, we taped the bottom of the bags and hoped for the best. Buyers stopped by the booth and picked up bags while I held my breath, hoping that the treats wouldn't fall out of the bottom and onto their shoes.

But that was the last straw for me. We had lost everything we had put into the business and then some. We had lost money entrusted to us by our friends and family. And, still, our bags had broken.

Everything I'd feared had happened, and it was even worse than I had imagined.

We didn't end up living in Pearl's basement, but it was close. Though I didn't go back to the city, I began doing some legal work from home for some of my old clients as Eric hustled to start our next venture.

I learned two lessons from Rover's failure. First, I can survive failure. It doesn't feel good, but it can be survived. Second, there are huge lessons to be learned. Now, looking back, I cherish both the experience and those lessons. I wouldn't trade the experience for anything.

So, the question is, how do you push past the fear of taking a risk? The answer is simple: Pearl's basement.

On today's walk, let your mind go to the worst possible scenario of what would happen if you chase the big dream or go after the big goal. Come face-to-face with what failure would look like. Reasonable failure. Realistic failure. Then make the decision to take your shot.

Walk # 29: MORK

One day, I created a word by accident: *mork*. I sent a colleague an email in which I intended to say, "Is this something we should do, or are we just creating more work?" But in my rush, I condensed the last two words and finished, "*...or are we just creating mork?*"

She responded, "By mork, do you mean *more work*?"

In that moment, I realized that the concept of work that is not essential to your goals or happiness deserves its own word.

Mork.

Mork refers to work, projects, and commitments that contribute to neither our goals nor our happiness. It is work that we feel we are "supposed" to do. Or projects that we've agreed to do even though we didn't want to and probably should have said no to in the first place.

For example, Sarah is a working mom of two young girls. Her husband is building his accounting practice and she is a speech pathologist who also teaches at a local college two nights a week. They are burning it at both ends, struggling to get the pieces of the puzzle to fit. By the time Sarah got home from work and found the signup sheet for the upcoming 4th grade Thanksgiving feast in her inbox, all the "easy" tasks had been taken. Paper plates, forks, knives, and spoons? Check. Water? Check. Tablecloths? Check.

But, there was still room in the dessert column. Quickly, Sarah checked the box for brownies. She would bring brownies.

The night before the Thanksgiving feast, Sarah was up until 2:00 AM baking brownies because she didn't want to be the mom who brought store-bought brownies to the Thanksgiving feast. She didn't want the other moms to think she didn't care enough to bake brownies from scratch. She didn't want to endure the silent judgment she feared, and was sure would come. Most importantly, she didn't want to be, in her own mind, the kind of mom who didn't prioritize her daughter's 4th grade Thanksgiving feast. She didn't want to take shortcuts.

Instead, Sarah took the afternoon off from work and showed up at the 4th grade Thanksgiving feast exhausted and bearing a big platter of brownies, which she deposited on the dessert table. "Oh," Sarah commented to another mom who was placing a platter of big, soft chocolate chip cookies on the table, "those look great."

The other mom smiled brightly. "Costco," she said and walked off to sit down next to her son.

Now, baking brownies from scratch for your daughter's 4th grade Thanksgiving feast might not be *mork* for everyone. Perhaps you love to bake. Perhaps brownies are your jam. Perhaps the day before the feast happened to be a day that was open on your calendar. Perhaps your homemade brownies are your daughter's most favorite thing in the world, and it would mean the world to her that you made them for her and her classmates.

But for Sarah, on that day, baking brownies from scratch was mork.

Not all work, projects, or efforts are created equal. We all have too much on our plates. Everyone commits to doing too much. Everyone feels pressed for time and like we are always running ten minutes—or ten hours—behind. Don't we? Perhaps there are those of you out there thinking, *Nope, I only commit to the things that are essential, and I have my life balanced perfectly.* If that's you, please call me, I need to hear your secrets.

For the rest of us, we have limited bandwidth. We only have so many productive hours in the day, and we need to work harder to determine what is important or what is just mork. If it's mork, let's work hard to be okay with saying (even if it is just saying it to yourself), "Nope, I'm not going to _____. It's not essential to my goals and it won't contribute to my happiness. It's mork, and I'm not doing it."

Yup, repeat after me: "It's mork, and I'm not doing it." Doesn't that feel good?

On today's walk, think about things that are currently on your "to do" list that might be mork. Ask yourself: *is that task essential to my goals or will it contribute to my happiness?*

Walk # 30: Don't Watch the Replay

In the final playoff game of Super Bowl LIII, the Los Angeles Rams played the New Orleans Saints. The winning team would go to the Super Bowl and along with that honor would come bragging rights, millions of dollars for the players, and huge economic benefits for the winning team's city.

Though I'm the daughter of a coach, I'm not a huge football fan. But nevertheless, I was watching that particular playoff game with a few friends. I have a soft spot for the New Orleans Saints because my lifetime BFF (we've been friends since we were two) lives there, and because of the hours I spent watching the huddles of people taking refuge inside their dome after the devastation wrought by Hurricane Katrina.

The score was 20-20 with less than two minutes to play. Drew Brees, the New Orleans Saints' quarterback, threw a pass to teammate Tommylee Lewis. But before Lewis could get his hands on the ball, he was taken out by the Rams' Nickell Robey-Colman. It was classic, unequivocal pass interference. Even I knew that. Yet somehow, the officials missed it and the Rams went on to compete in Super Bowl LIII. It's been dubbed the "worst call that was never called in NFL history." The Saints were robbed of their Super Bowl and the evidence was clear to anyone who watched the replay—which means pretty much everyone. The NFL issued a formal apology. People called for the playoff game to be replayed. It was a mess. In the end, the NFL stuck with their call, and people, for the most part, got over their anger and moved on.

Many of us watch the replay of our mistakes over and over again. They keep us from falling asleep or play on a loop when we wake up in the middle of the night. We replay stupid things we've said, the opportunities we've blown, and the ways we've disappointed people. We think about the ice cream we ate, the test we bombed, or the moment when we lost our temper with our toddler.

I've often wondered about the value of these replays. Are they necessary to prevent us from repeating our mistakes? Do we learn from them or do they merely keep us from moving forward and prevent us from taking risks?

Unfortunately, the answer lies somewhere in between. If we move forward without acknowledging our mistakes, we miss a vital opportunity to learn, grow, and improve. If we are immune from regret, we run the risk of blowing through life without concern for the people we hurt along the way, and we miss the chance to reflect and grow.

The problem lies when we don't use the replays to learn and grow and instead we use them to torture ourselves. When we get caught up in the replay loop, our thoughts turn from "what can I learn or, better yet, how can I repair the situation?" to "I suck." We can easily go from acknowledging one mistake to replaying an entire loop of other instances when we've screwed up. Finding the right balance, especially in the middle of the night, is very difficult. But...it is possible.

Give yourself permission to watch the replay. Don't try to shut it down, at least not the first time. If it wants to be watched, it will be watched.

Look at the situation and consider whether or not there is something you can do to fix it. I'll give you an example. I went live via social media in front of 500 people to honor the top local publisher in our company as the Publisher of the Year. While live, in front of hundreds and hundreds of people, I mentioned some personal challenges that had been encountered by Elena, another member of our business community. I mentioned her by name. It was completely inappropriate and as I got into bed that night, it took away all of the joy that I had felt when bestowing the honor of Publisher of the Year on a very deserving woman. All I could think about was how badly I had overstepped.

At about 11:00 PM, I grabbed my phone from beside my bed and sent a heartfelt apology to Elena. Finally, I was able to sleep.

If you are watching the replay of something you can fix—or at least attempt to fix—then set out to fix it. That should stop the replay.

Sometimes, our replays stem from long ago, or things that can't be corrected for whatever reason. Those replays are trickier to manage. These two things can help.

First, ask yourself if there's anything to be learned. If so, write it down. For instance, I have discovered that the stupidest things I say in meetings always come at the end. If I'm having an important meeting, the meeting can be going great but in the last five minutes, I am likely to say something really stupid. So, I've strived to learn that lesson and, as a meeting begins to wind down, I become hyper-vigilant about what I say. If there are lessons to be learned from your replay, learn them.

Second, don't catastrophize the replay. That one piece of chocolate cake does not mean you are destined to be overweight forever, the one blow up at your toddler does not mean she is destined for a lifetime of therapy, and the one botched meeting does not mean your career is finished. Do not let one replay trigger the loop of all the other times you've screwed up.

On today's walk, think about how often you replay moments that you wish you could change, and consider whether or not there are any replays that you can, and should, repair.

Walk # 31: The Power of Yet

The "growth mindset" has swept the world in everything from parenting and education to professional development and preschool over the past several years.

The concept was first articulated—and the phrase first coined—by researcher Carol Dweck thirty years ago. Dweck had studied the behavior of thousands of children and discovered that children who believed that they could get smarter were the ones who did the work to achieve more. This reinforced their belief that they could learn and achieve, which reinforced their willingness to do the work in a positive, self-perpetuating cycle. Conversely, children who believed that their capabilities and talents were fixed, and therefore limited, were more likely to be frustrated and give up.

In other words, growth mindset means believing in the power to learn, grow, and improve at just about everything. Research shows that merely holding that belief empowers you to learn, grow, and improve.

Okay, sure, some people have more innate talent at some things than other things. If you are 4 feet 11 inches, a career as a professional women's basketball player is likely not in your future. If (like me) you can't carry a tune, then opera is probably not where you will make your mark in the world. But with the exception of some, pretty much all skills can be developed, all things can be learned, and—with enough desire, dedication, and grit—most things can be mastered.

This is awesome because evolution has wired a desire to learn into our DNA. That is clear from the little spark of joy we get when we master a new skill, learn a smart trick, or accomplish a special goal. Yet as adults, we often halt our journey. Perhaps because we were told as children that we were no good at something. Perhaps because we believe that, as adults, we are supposed to have the answers. Perhaps because we don't dedicate time to learning and developing new skills.

Everything can be learned through training. You have the capacity to learn, develop, and grow throughout your life. In fact, research has shown that people who continue lifelong learning live longer. Yup, learning new skills throughout your life will literally prolong your life.

In my work with women, I remain shocked by the sheer number of times I hear women say, "I'm not good at this or that." Interestingly enough, this is not something you hear from men, though I suppose that's a topic for another book. Anyway, every time you say, "I'm not good at X," you are cutting yourself off from possibility.

There is a simple way to begin to develop a growth mindset. Simply add the word "yet" to the end of any sentence or thought that begins with "I'm not good at..." or "I can't do..."

"I'm not good at cooking... yet"

"I'm not good at writing... yet."

"I'm not good at sales... yet."

"I'm not good at double unders... yet."

Take Caroline. As a senior executive with a bright future at our company, she had a strong desire to improve her leadership skills. With leadership often comes the ability to address a group of people—especially through public speaking. We were standing in front of the room at our annual conference in front of 150 people when I handed her the mic and whispered, "Announce the winners of this morning's contest." She looked at me, took a deep breath and began her public speaking journey. She wasn't good at public speaking until she was.

On today's walk, think about the things that you want to do, be, or accomplish and add the word "yet" to each of them in your mind.

Walk # 32: The 3 Fs

On our last walk, we thought about the importance of embracing a growth mindset and the power of "yet." Today, I want to think about what specific skills we need to develop to help us reach our goals.

For pretty much my entire life, any time I was wrestling with a challenge, my dad asked, "Who can help you?" When Eric was striving to crack the Top 20 in the annual CrossFit master's competition, my dad asked, "Where can he get some coaching?" When business was hitting a challenge, my dad asked, "Who can help you figure it out?" When we were working through challenges with our kids, my dad asked, "Where can you get some advice?"

This makes sense, since my dad spent his life coaching kids in school, soccer, track, and life. My dad is also very humble. Though he has brilliant social skills and a unique ability to get to the heart of people, he will always admit when there are people who know more than he does about a particular subject. As such, he is always open to advice and learning. In fact, at ninety years old, he just hired his first personal trainer to help him navigate new equipment that was introduced at his gym.

When Eric and I married, we discovered we shared a love of books of all kinds and we developed a little relationship shorthand for when we were ready to take on a new challenge: "There's gotta' be a book for that."

Renovating a bathroom? There's gotta' be a book for that.

Starting a media company? There's gotta' be a book for that.

Selling that company? Yup, there was a book for that, too.

But here's what we haven't been as good at: deliberately identifying and cultivating skills we want to develop or skills that we should strive to develop for our future. We are usually so caught up in the moment and mired in the responsibilities of our lives that the act of consciously creating a plan to develop specific skills has never been part of what we do. Until now.

At all times, you—and I—should be working on what I've coined the "F3 Skills": Fitness, Future, and Fun.

Skill F1: Fitness. Now I don't mean working on your double unders or building your biceps. I mean fitness for your current life. Ask yourself, *if I could wave a magic wand and master one skill that would make my life better right now, it would be...*

Say, for instance, that you work in customer service for a bank. What new skill would most impact your ability to excel in your job? Are you a SAHM mom? What parenting skill are you struggling with? The challenge is to look at the roles and responsibilities with which you are currently charged and identify the one skill that would have the greatest impact on your ability—your fitness—to perform better.

Skill F2: Future. This one is challenging because it requires you to look into a crystal ball. At the same time, you have to remember that wherever you are right now is going to change with time. Babies will grow up and head off to school, school-aged kids will run off to college. Jobs will change. Houses will be sold and new ones bought. As they say, change is the only constant in life. The good news is that change opens up an entire world of opportunity for you to prepare for those changes. Yet, so few people actually stop to really consider what and where they want to go next, much less what skills they could develop to help them. That's F2: what skills can you develop *now* that will give you the greatest chance for success *then?* Look ahead three to five years. Where will you be? What skills will help you succeed at that stage? Start working on developing those skills now and you'll be surprised by how prepared you are for the future.

Skill F3: Fun. You know how much I believe in the power of fun. But did you know that developing skills around something you enjoy raises the fun quotient? Riding horses. Knitting. Cooking. Painting. Completing your first 5k or improving your time on your tenth. At all times, you should be intentionally working on developing one skill simply for the joy of it. This is not indulgent, selfish, or a waste of time. More fun means more happiness and more happiness means a better, more fulfilling life.

Identify your 3Fs, then make a deliberate plan for developing them. For example, at the front of my goalpost notebook, I have written down my 3Fs. I treat each month as a fresh start and make a plan for building upon each of my 3Fs. How you develop each of your 3F skills depends a bit on what they are, but there are many, many options. So many options...

As of this writing, there are 28 million podcast episodes, most of which are free, that inform and educate on more topics than you can imagine.

There are webinars—free and paid for—on topics that cover and educate on just about everything you can think of.

There are apps that teach new languages or how to take better pictures.

There are countless free videos that teach knitting, painting, or even how to bake a wedding cake.

There are college courses, both online and in person.

And, as I've always said, whatever you are looking to learn or master, there's probably a book for that.

Walk # 33: Get High on Helping

Yesterday I was at the beach watching a dad take his three-year-old into the ocean. As soon as the little boy touched the water, he was off, his little arms and legs motoring along. Within seconds, he was five feet away. The dad tore off his t-shirt, tossed it to the beach, and went after his bobbing toddler. The shirt landed on the sand, so close to the water's edge that one big wave was sure to sweep it away. I got up from my beach chair, grabbed the dad's t-shirt and moved it out of the reach of the coming tide. It was a tiny gesture that went completely unnoticed. But as I walked back to my chair, I felt just a tiny bit happier.

That's no surprise. There is ample and compelling research that helping others lights up the pleasure center in our brain and delivers a little shot of the three happiness hormones: oxytocin, serotonin, and dopamine. This feeling of joy brought on by helping others has been dubbed the "helper's high" and brain mapping has shown it is a real thing. *How awesome is that?* Helping others makes us feel good. As Dr. Eva Ritvo wrote in *The Neuroscience of Giving,* "[h]umans are social animals, so it is no surprise that we are wired to help one another." In fact, this instinct is so powerful that there is evidence that people who regularly volunteer actually live longer than those who don't.

Getting your daily dose of helper's high is pretty simple. Sure, you can spend Thanksgiving serving dinner in a shelter or volunteer eight hours a week with at-risk kids—both of which are awesome—but you can also help an elderly woman with her grocery bags, give up your seat to someone who looks like they need it more than you do, or buy coffee for the guy in line behind you. Or, as I did just this morning, bring your husband his morning coffee in bed.

Not only will these little acts of kindness give you a dose of helper's high, they change the way others both react to and treat you. Usually, though not always, an act of kindness is met with a smile and a "thank you," and since smiles are contagious, the more people smile at you, the more you will smile too.

Your small acts of kindness can also have a ripple effect on others. A person's entire mood can change when they experience an act of kindness.

As I've always told my kids, "You have the power to make the people around you feel good or feel bad, and which you choose defines the kind of person you will be." Remarkably—at least in my experience—it doesn't matter if you are doing a kind and generous act in part with a goal of making yourself feel better. So, if you think donating your time at a local soup kitchen, reading at a nursing home, walking puppies at a local shelter, bringing your partner coffee in bed, or simply smiling at the slow-moving woman behind the ticket counter will make you feel good, that's a good enough reason to do it.

On today's walk, think about working to consciously change the way you go through the rest of the day. Look for the opportunities to commit acts of kindness and share compassion. And then notice how those acts affect you.

Walk # 34: Can I Have a Do-over?

Eric and I have been married for more than 20 years. We've worked side-by-side building four businesses, raising two kids and three dogs, building a house, and taken countless family ski trips—all recipes for stress. And believe me, we've had our fair share: a dent in the door frame from the cereal bowl I threw at him during one early argument is a testament to the fact that it hasn't always been easy. In fact, relationships are rarely easy. But we work at them daily by speaking our minds, communicating as honestly as possible, and by reminding ourselves "I choose you" daily.

But there's one relationship hack that we developed early on in both our personal and professional lives that I know has helped us stay on track: do-overs.

Last night Eric was snippy with me. I have no idea why, though I think it had something to do with something I said at dinner about one of his friends. Or maybe he was just tired. Or maybe he had a stomachache. Or maybe he was thinking about the fact that our son leaves for college in a week. Whatever it was, he was cranky, and I was the recipient.

Eric hates when I call him cranky or ask him what's wrong, but I hate not knowing what's bothering him. So I ask. And that makes him crankier. See the cycle?

Anyway, after dinner, we were in our little office both catching up on some emails, and I asked, "What's bugging you?" And I got my head bitten off. I looked at him and said, "I didn't do anything to deserve that; this one is on you." I went upstairs to get ready for bed. A few minutes later, he followed.

"Can I have a do-over, please?" I took a deep breath because I was still stinging a bit from having my head bit off.

"Of course," I said. And that was the end of it.

Have you ever been in an argument with your partner, and, at some point deep in the argument forgotten what you are truly arguing about, or realized whatever you are arguing about is really stupid? Or, have you ever snapped at your partner even though you know in your heart, they are not the cause of whatever is bugging you?

Those are the moments you can ask for a do-over. It is shorthand for "I love you, I'm sorry, and this is not worth arguing about." All three of those conditions must be met before you can call a do-over.

First, a request for a do-over must start from a place of love. In fact, requests for do-overs often start with "I love you; can I have a do-over?"

Second, it must come with true acceptance of responsibility and a sense of apology. Now, that doesn't mean you are accepting full responsibility or implying that the entire argument or situation is entirely your fault. It always takes two to argue. But it is one person saying, "I'm sorry for my part."

Finally, a do-over can only end an argument that's not worth arguing about. Arguments that reflect deeper problems or more persistent problems aren't subject to do-overs. Do-overs are never an excuse to treat your partner badly or abusively. You do not get a free pass for things that are important, abusive, or persistent.

However, in relationships, sometimes you are snappy or short for no reason. Sometimes you find yourself in an argument with no purpose, about something you don't really care about all that much, yet somehow got sucked into the argument for the sake of arguing.

We've discovered that do-overs work pretty well with teenage kids too. Teenagers are the kings and queens of snappy behavior for no reason. Truly, research suggests that they can't help themselves—hormones they can't control make them cranky. We taught our kids about do-overs and occasionally, after a particularly obnoxious teen encounter, they will come to us and say, "Can I have a do-over?"

Yup, you sure can.

On today's walk, think about whether or not there are times when you and your partner find yourselves arguing about something fairly minor or when "winning" the argument becomes the goal when you don't really care about the underlying issue all that much. In other words, could you have implemented a do-over?

Walk # 35: I Was Dumped by My Best Friend

My husband and I had dream friends: they had kids the same age as our kids and, remarkably, we adored both parents. We spent holidays together and traveled together. Jenny and I walked in the woods with our dogs—yup, even our dogs were friends. I spent hours on the phone with her when her mother was ill. We talked about everything—relationships, kids, brothers, sisters, and business.

We had dinner plans with another family when that morning I received a strange text from Jenny about her daughter.

"Is everything okay?" I texted back.

"It's not a conversation for text message," she replied.

So, I did what any friend would do on a Saturday morning—I picked up the phone and called her. What I heard was a laundry list of frustrations being encountered by the mom of a thirteen-year-old girl. I asked questions and, I thought, offered support and encouragement. After all, I was right there with her, right? Every kid is not the same, but thirteen-year-old girls are, well, thirteen-year-old girls.

"You know," she said in a manner that seemed out of the blue to me. "You sound very curt, and I don't appreciate your tone."

My tone? I'm listening, asking questions, seeking to understand. "I'm sorry," I said. "I'm trying to understand what happened."

I suppose what she was looking for was a whole lot more of "*you're right, her behavior sounds awful*" but so far, I hadn't heard that—I just heard a typical litany of complaints about a thirteen-year-old girl who wouldn't clean her room and sometimes tried to play one parent off of the other.

"You are very matter of fact. That's just how you are, but that's not what I need this morning."

Jenny ended the conversation abruptly and, despite several attempts by me to reach out, it appeared our friendship had been summarily and unilaterally terminated.

I was hurt, confused, and sad.

My guess is that this has happened to you at some point in your life too. In the State of Mom Report, we discovered that 73% of the 2,300 women who responded admit to being lonely, 20% don't feel they have any friends, and a whopping 70% don't feel they have enough time to spend with the friends they do have. Add to it that several respondents noted personal thoughts along the lines of: "I'd rather stick to myself. Been done wrong too many times."

I hear you. Like all relationships, friendships are tricky. Like any relationship, friendships end in all kinds of ways. Some suddenly and dramatically, while others cool over time. Sometimes a move, or a new job, or a new relationship, or some other change in your lifestyle puts you out of sync with a friend. Sometimes a friendship simply runs its course. Or sometimes you get dumped and don't know why.

So, what do you do when you've been dumped by a friend?

First, if you are going to grow from any experience, you have to look at it objectively. It's important to strive to understand if you played a role in the relationship's end and how things could have played out differently. Perhaps I could have been more understanding or compassionate with Jenny. Or perhaps she was upset about something else entirely or something that I had or hadn't done. Perhaps she was struggling in more ways than I knew, and there would not have been anything I could do about it.

Second, sometimes an argument with a friend is just that, an argument, and the relationship can—and should—be resolved. Do not walk away on principle or pride. People falter, fail, and argue. If the relationship is important enough to you, and it can be saved, you must do whatever it takes to save it. Make the call. Offer the apology. Accept responsibility.

Finally, sometimes you have to accept that perhaps the friendship, even if it was important to you, was not meant to continue. And that's okay. Not every relationship is meant to be forever. If that's the case, accept it, make peace with it, and move on.

On today's walk, think about any friendships that you would like to repair and any past friendships you need to mourn and release.

● ● ●

Walk # 36: The Other People

There are three categories of people who don't make your life better and identifying them is the first step in deciding how much influence they have on your life.

Category one: the dream killers.

For as long as I can remember, writing is how I've processed my thoughts and expressed myself. In elementary school, I created characters and made up stories. In high school, I processed all my angst with pen and paper. In college, I first wrote with the hope of encouraging people to think more deeply and act more intentionally.

So it was no surprise that at the ripe old age of 23, I decided to write a book. It just so happened that there was a paralegal at the law firm where I worked who was also an inspiring writer, though she was far, far further ahead in her journey than I was. Rumor had it that she had a completed manuscript and an agent. One day, I found myself sitting beside her in the library, strangely empty of anyone else. "I've decided to write a book," I said. "I know you're a writer, do you have any advice?"

"Don't bother," she said. "You don't have any life experience. No one under 30 has anything valuable to say."

Yup, a dream killer. A person who feels compelled to pull you back and discourage your dreams. Often, it is because they are afraid of what your success would mean for them. Sometimes, they are trying to protect you from failure. Occasionally, it is just because they are mean.

Category two: the Eeyores.

Karen and I used to work out together three times a week. We'd meet in the lobby of our office building after work and walk the six blocks to the gym, catching up on our day before changing in the locker room and heading to the treadmills where I would gratefully slip on my headphones to tune out her constant stream of negativity. Invariably, her day had sucked, her boss was a jerk, and her boyfriend had disappointed her again. She didn't feel like working out. The weather was too hot, too cold, too humid, or too dry. Karen could find the bad in every situation and relished sharing it with anyone who would listen.

There are people who find the dark cloud in an otherwise clear sky, see every glass as half empty, and feel compelled to share their negativity with you. Sometimes they want you to share in their unhappiness, but often they just can't help themselves because negative is how they see the world. I call them the Eeyores.

Category three: the egoists.

Now, I don't believe in keeping score. Really, I don't. But one day last week, I was on the phone with an old friend with whom I catch up with every few weeks. As she droned on about every moment of her life since we had spoken last, I glanced at the clock: 3:46 PM. As the conversation began to wind down at 4:20 PM, my friend, for the first time, asked, "So how are you?"

"I'm okay," I replied. "Work is really challenging right now and I'm a little worried … I'm not sleeping well," I concluded.

"Oh, I hear you," she replied. "I woke up at four-thirty this morning and couldn't get back to sleep." What followed was another eight minutes of her work challenges before I ended the call as graciously as possible. Yup, I call them the egoists.

We all have these people in our worlds. Some books, therapists, and well-meaning others will advise simply ejecting them from our lives. Sometimes that's the right choice (see, ex-husband), but sometimes these are people who, for one reason or another, remain in our life. Consider a self-absorbed sister, a friend who is going through a rough patch, or a mother who feels it is her job to point out every flaw in your plans.

Though we can't always remove people from our lives, we can develop clarity around their nature and decide how much influence they get to have.

On today's walk, think about the influence that the people close to you have on your life. Do you have a dream killer, Eeyore, or egoist in your life? If so, are these people who can be removed? If not, simply seeing them for who they are can often help reduce their influence.

● ● ●

Walk # 37: Don't be a Dream Killer

On our last walk, we explored three categories of people who have an influence on our lives so that we need to consciously limit our time spent with them. On today's walk, we are going to check in with our own behavior to be sure that we aren't a Dream Killer, Eeyore, or Egoist.

My friend Caroline has always wanted to open a boutique filled with perfectly curated fair-trade clothing from around the world. Beautiful flowing cotton dresses from India, intricately crocheted sweaters from Peru, and stunning jewelry from Africa. She had talked about this dream for as long as I've known her and when a perfect location became available in the middle of town, she wanted to go for it. The problem was that Caroline already had a full-time job, a one-hour commute and a daughter in high school. Her plan wasn't to quit her job, but to open the store in her "spare time" and find someone fabulous to manage the day-to-day.

There were several potential problems with this plan. First, she wasn't in the financial position to take a huge risk for the fun of it. This wasn't going to be a hobby, this had to be a serious business—the store *had* to work. Second, I know first-hand how challenging it is to start any new business, so the idea of trying to do that on top of her responsibilities as a full-time senior executive seemed more than a bit daunting. Third, finding that "fabulous person" to manage the day-to-day was going to be really, really hard. Maybe impossible.

On walk after walk (Caroline is one of my favorite walking partners), she would share her vision and her plan. She'd talk about the beautiful things she would import and the beautiful boutique she'd create. She'd brainstorm display ideas and we'd kick around marketing plans. Before we knew it, she signed a lease and got to work. That was when things got real. Our walking conversations turned to how hard it was to launch a new business while commuting and working and raising a family. In my effort to empathize, I would say things like, *"I don't know how you are doing it all,"* or *"Girl, you have too much on your plate,"* or, worst of all, *"Are you sure this isn't just too much?"*

My intentions were good, but one morning, I heard the words coming out of my mouth and realized that I was being a dream killer. *Why?*

Because I cared about her and I didn't want to see her add more pressure to an already stressful life. Nevertheless, once she signed the lease and committed, that was not what she needed to hear. Consciously, I made the decision to change how I responded when she spoke of her challenges from *"That all sounds too hard"* to *"You've got this, how can I help?"*

At times we can all find ourselves slipping into the role of Dream Killer, Eeyore, or Egoist with our friends, our children, and ourselves. Like when we meet an old friend for a glass of wine and launch into every challenging thing that happened during our day. Or when we unload a list of complaints on our partner. Or when we let a litany of negative thoughts swirl around our brain when we lay in bed at the end of the day. Or when we tell our children to be careful.

On today's walk, think about which of these tendencies is most typical for you. Consider the last time you had the opportunity to encourage someone's dream and ask yourself if you did. Or the last time you chose to focus on the negative rather than the positive. Think about the things you are telling yourself about your dreams and your goals. Remember the last time you responded to a friend's challenge with a story of your own challenge, rather than really listening.

And then, decide that you will not be a Dream Killer, Eeyore, or Egoist.

● ● ●

Walk # 38: We are Fighting Biology

Before I leave for any trip, the following things always go through my head: Will I die in a fiery plane crash? Will my house get robbed? Will one of my parents get sick and need me? Will someone get hurt? If I'm leaving on a vacation, I add: I have too much to do. People work harder than I do. Many people don't have the luxury of vacation, and I'm being selfish. If I'll be traveling without my family, I add: What if the kids need me? Wait, the kids do need me; they need me all the time.

I wonder, *should I cancel* and invariably answer, *yes, I should probably cancel*. Occasionally I do cancel, but more often than not, I get on the plane. Travel isn't the only time I catastrophize (yup, that's a real word). According to PsychCentral.com:

"Catastrophizing is an irrational thought a lot of us have in believing that something is far worse than it actually is. Catastrophizing can generally take two different forms: making a catastrophe out of a current situation and imagining making a catastrophe out of a future situation."

If we have a bad month in business, I think, *Sales are not going to turn around. I'm going to have to lay off members of my team and that will suck. And then things will only get worse. What if we lose the business and then lose our home?*

Yup, one bad month of sales can lead my mind to the possibility of losing my house and moving into Pearl's basement. And don't even get me started on all of the terrible things I imagine can happen to my kids whenever they are out of my sight.

This tendency to catastrophize aligns with our natural tendencies. Our biology, what experts refer to as our inborn "negativity bias." And that makes sense—if we didn't have an internal voice warning us about the risks inherent in leaving the cave, we'd all have been eaten by saber-toothed tigers (*Smithsonian* magazine recently reported that it is possible that saber-toothed tigers did, in fact, roam the earth at the same time as our human ancestors). For most of us, once we become parents, these instincts kick into high gear because now we don't just have ourselves to protect. We have our cubs to keep safe, too.

Taking risks, taking chances, and straying from the cave require that we recognize our negativity bias and any tendency we have to catastrophize. We have to work to look at situations with objectivity so we can make a realistic determination of the risk.

On today's walk, think about any tendency you have to catastrophize. When presented with a situation, a challenge or an opportunity, do you jump to "worst-case scenario"? Do you continue down that path to even more extreme "what ifs"? That's okay, that's your biology at work.

Recognize it for what it is and thank your beautiful brain for striving to keep you and your pack safe. But then, take a step back and ground yourself in reality. Yes, there are risks, but how likely is that worst-case scenario? Are those risks worth holding you back from pursuing your dreams and goals and from chasing your best, biggest, and brightest life? Usually not.

● ● ●

Walk # 39: The Problem with Pi Day

March 14 can be written as 3.14—the mathematical constant of a circle's circumference to its diameter—a magic number in the math world. So, March 14 is often called "Pi Day." To celebrate last Pi Day, I ate apple pie for breakfast. Then I ate a little more for lunch because, well, because it was there, and it was delicious, and the day was shot already, right? Dinner was a big plate of spaghetti with butter and parmesan cheese. Emphasis on big.

I take nutrition pretty seriously. I believe in the importance of fueling my body well because that is the only way that I will feel good and have the energy to do all of the things I want to do. Nutrition enables me to bounce out of bed ready to chase my kids and my dreams. It is what powers me to pick up and put down heavy things in the gym, walk four miles, and still have the energy to write my daily 600 words. I know that food is fuel.

Yet, some days, nutrition goes south, and more often than not, a crappy eating day starts with a crappy breakfast. That's part biology and part mentality.

For me, what I eat for breakfast—or don't eat—determines the rest of my day from a nutrition standpoint. If I eat carbs for breakfast—even high-quality multigrain, nutritious carbs—by 11:00 AM I'm starving. And not that *Hmmmm, I feel like a snack* hungry, that gnawing *must have food now* hunger. For me, breakfast has to be protein-based, even if what I think I want is oatmeal. Over the years, breakfast has changed. For years it was egg whites with spinach and mushrooms and a little cheese thrown into a pan. These days, it is a breakfast smoothie into which I try to toss the equivalent of an entire salad, a bit of fruit, and a big scoop of plant-based protein powder.

But, oh how I love donuts. And blueberry muffins. And warm cinnamon rolls. But if that's how I start the day, I often end the day with the aforementioned spaghetti, washed down with a bowl of ice cream.

Eating a crappy breakfast also has a mental component because, for many of us, when we feel we've already "slipped up," we tend to write off the entire day. This is, frankly, kinda silly because even a Boston Kreme donut from Dunkin' Donuts has only 300 calories. Certainly, they aren't good calories, but adding an extra 300 calories to your day before 9:00 AM is definitely, positively not a reason to write off the day. And yet so often we do. Interestingly, a Starbucks latte has 190 calories and I suspect that for many, indulging in a latte is far, far less likely to mentally derail your nutrition intentions for the day then a donut.

What you eat for breakfast does matter, to your blood sugar, your body, and your mind. Each morning provides a fresh opportunity to set up your day for success. It is also the most hectic time of the day for most of us, with little ones bursting with morning energy and bigger ones who have to be prepped and sent off to school, all at the same time that you are preparing for your own day, commute, work, commitments and all. It is not the time to be figuring out breakfast on the fly.

Now many of us know the benefits of meal planning for dinner, we but rarely consider meal planning for breakfast. But I say, let's consider it.

Let's meal-plan breakfast.

Begin with a basic goal: no crap. Minimal sugar, nothing processed, no white carbs. Here are six options. Because I prefer to make as few decisions as possible, especially in the midst of my hectic morning, I can happily eat the exact same thing pretty much every morning. Once I decide, once it becomes a habit, it sticks, often for years.

- A morning smoothie. These days, I manage to eat the equivalent of an entire salad before 8:00. Into my beloved Nutribullet goes almond or soymilk, a scoop of plant-based protein powder, three ice cubes, a huge handful of kale, a smaller handful of spinach, an even smaller handful of sprouts, half a banana, a large tablespoon of avocado, a hunk of ginger and whatever fruit I have in the fridge or freezer.

- Egg white omelet with black beans, spinach, mushrooms, diced tomatoes and a sprinkle of feta cheese. If you can avoid the cheese, even better, but for me, eggs need a little cheese. That's just how it is.

- Sliced banana with peanut butter. This is not the best option, but some days it is all a crazy-busy mama bear can manage. Plus, it beats a Dunkin Donuts maple glazed donut.

- Two hard-boiled eggs with hummus.

- Greek yogurt with berries and just a sprinkle of granola for crunch (beware the granola, it can be a sugar-loaded mess, but a sprinkle for flavor and crunch won't kill ya).

- Egg muffins. Break out your muffin tin, whisk up eggs, spinach, mushrooms, and, if you must, cheese. Add some diced turkey bacon. Fill the muffin cups and bake for about fifteen to twenty minutes. And here's the thing: these muffins will keep for a few days, so bake 'em up on Sunday and you should be set through Wednesday.

The bottom line is this: do not start your day with crap. Apple pie for breakfast? No good. Egg whites with spinach and a handful of black beans or a protein shake with kale, spinach, protein powder, and half a banana? Good. Decide right now what you are going to eat for breakfast each morning for the rest of the week.

Walk # 40: Build Your Starting Block

My dad was a competitive sprinter, meaning that the majority of his running success was predicated on races that lasted less than a minute. When the race is that short and that intense, one of the things that separates the victor from those in second, third, and even last place is the start. Runners crouch down at the starting line, place their heels against the starting block and wait for the gun to go off. When it does, they come off of that block with tremendous focus and intensity and give the race everything they've got. They end gasping for air.

Any sprinter will tell you that how they come off the starting block can decide the race. To give your day everything you've got, you need your own starting block. A way to brace and focus yourself so that you can launch into the day's race with everything you've got.

You need a morning routine.

Now before we talk about what it should be, let's talk about what it shouldn't be. Your morning shouldn't begin with you hitting the snooze bar five times. It shouldn't start with you rolling over, picking up your phone and scrolling Facebook, Instagram, or email. It shouldn't include a glazed donut, glass of sweet tea, or bottle of Coke. Whenever possible, it should start before your kids wake up.

Your morning routine should be a series of steps you take each morning that prepares you physically, mentally, emotionally, and spiritually for the day to come. It doesn't need to be complicated and it doesn't have to take long—fifteen minutes is good and thirty minutes is better.

Your perfect morning routine is likely to be a little bit different from mine and it will likely change and evolve as you discover what works for you.

Here's the first morning routine I developed three years ago, which I stayed with for about year.

- Pour a glass of water, which I drink and refill once or twice.
- Pour a cup of coffee, which I drink as well (the coffee pot's timer is set the night before, and the smell of coffee brewing helps propel me out of bed).

- Make an entry in my gratitude journal (I use a simple gratitude app).
- Exercise just a little to get the blood going and wake up my central nervous system (ten easy squats, a thirty-second plank, a couple of stretches).
- Journal for five minutes, which felt awkward and forced—I'm not one for journaling—but I wanted to see if that routine helped me clarify my mood, thoughts, or intentions for the day.

Over time, my morning routine has become incredibly precious. It has grown to forty-five minutes, and I cherish every second of it. Here's what my morning routine looks like right now. And yup, I did these things this morning, in this order.

1. Pour (and drink!) a glass of water.
2. Make an entry in my gratitude journal.
3. Stretch my calves, hips, and lower back (these are the three spots that I need to stretch every day).
4. Meditate for ten minutes.
5. Read five pages of a book that inspires me or teaches me something and take notes as I read.
6. Review my goals for the month or the year (I review monthly goals during the month and my year-long goals at the start of the month) and measure my progress.
7. Write a few sentences about what is most important for the day, or what I'm most excited about working on.
8. Ask myself, and write down, the single most important and valuable thing I can do that day.
9. Do not give up. Yup, I remind myself every single day not to give up on my dreams and my goals.

I keep this all organized on the inside front cover of my Goalpost notebook, which we'll dig into in detail of on our next walk. When I get to the end of the notebook and need to start a new one, I take a bit of time to consider what's working in my morning routine. *What might I want to change for the following few months?* Then I rewrite my morning routine on the inside front cover.

This is my starting block. These are the things I do daily to enable me to launch into the day and give it everything I've got. I don't think there is one single thing I do in my life that is more essential to my success than this.

If you do not have a morning routine—a true morning routine that you practice pretty much every day—today is the day you begin to create one.

On today's walk, think about how you start your day. Are you stressed? Tired? Rushed? Picture a morning routine that launches you into the day feeling productive, organized, and ready to roll. 'Cause tomorrow you are going to start that way.

Go.

● ● ●

Walk # 41: Your Goalpost

If you've ever played any sports, or watched any sports, you know that the goalpost is the target to which the team drives. Consider football. Bit by bit, yard by yard, players move toward the goalpost. They get tackled—sometimes brutally. They get pushed off course and shoved out of bounds. Sometimes, they miss a pass or fumble the ball. Occasionally, they trip.

Imagine if you will, what would happen if there was no goalpost, no clearly marked target. No end zone. When a player is pushed out of bounds, how much valuable time would it take for him to regain his focus and to figure out where he is going if he didn't have a thirty-foot target, visible from anywhere on the field, to head toward?

We all need our own personal goalpost. Something that crystallizes our goals and that we can see clearly and work toward every day.

Meet my Morning Goalpost.

I know, it sounds fancy, but it is nothing more than an inexpensive, spiral-bound 6" by 9" notebook. But it's the most important notebook in my life, and it will be in yours. I promise. Because it will be the place where you plant your stake in the ground and the playbook you use to drive toward it.

Here's how it works.

At the start of the year, I start a fresh Goalpost Notebook. This is where I articulate my goals for the year and my goals for each month, where I identify the 3F skills I'm working on at any given time, and where my morning routine lives.

Here's exactly how I set it up.

First, I write the start date on the front cover—because I usually go through three or four during the course of the year, I like to know the date on which I start and end each notebook.

Next, I turn to the inside cover and write down the nine steps of my Morning Routine because, even though I do them each day, I sometimes forget the order or leave things out. Besides, I don't want to have to re-member things in the morning or make any decisions because I'm always striving to conserve my decision-making capacity. So, it is easier to just flip open the front cover and work through the list.

As you know from our last walk, my current Morning Routine looks like this:

1. Drink water
2. Gratitude
3. Stretch
4. Meditate
5. Read 5 pages (and take notes)
6. Review goals/Measure progress
7. Write about today
8. Identify 3 MITs (Most Important Things for the day)
9. Do not give up

Below that, also in the front cover, I write my current 3Fs, the three skills I'm working on that we talked about on Walk #32:

Right now, those three skills are:

1F: Fitness: Writing

2F: Future: Public Speaking

3F: Fun: CrossFit

Then, on the first page, in block letters, I write my big goals for the year. I find that between five and ten goals are perfect—any fewer and I can't capture all of the key things I plan to accomplish that year, any more and my goal list runs the risk of becoming my "to do" list. It is critical that those goals are something I can measure rather than something subjective. For a while, I had a goal that read "create great content" but I realized there was no way to measure that and that means there is no way to know when I've crushed it.

My current year's goal list reads:

1. Complete and publish this book
2. Grow revenue by 20%
3. Create awesome weekly content including:
   a. Five Images
   b. One blog post
   c. Two videos
   d. One podcast
4. Send 100 thank you cards

5. Take a trip one-on-one with each of my kids
6. CrossFit:
   a. Complete 1 muscle up
   b. Link 30 double unders
   c. Deadlift 205 lbs
7. Do a TED Talk

On the next page, I write my goals for the current month. Those monthly goals are incremental steps toward my bigger goals. Once again, I keep them to no more than five or six so they don't become an overwhelming "to do" list, and if I've learned anything at all, it is that focusing on just a few specific goals is critical, especially for a self-confessed "idea junkie" with a monkey mind, like me.

My goals for this month include:

1. Complete the first draft of all 99 sections of this book
2. Link fifteen double unders
3. Release the new app
4. Prepare all of the materials for an upcoming team summit
5. Schedule three white space days
6. Recharge and have fun

I added number 6 because I recognized that I was feeling burned out and overworked at the end of last month.

Then I get to work.

Before I go to bed, I place my Goalpost, the book I am currently reading, the notebook I'm using to take notes on that book, and my headphones (for my morning meditation) on my chair.

When I wake up, I flip the switch on the coffee pot and flip open my Goalpost to my morning routine.

When I read #6, "Review Goals and Measure Progress" I flip to the start of the current month and take a look at how I'm doing. Then, it is on to #7 and I capture just a few sentences in which I set an intention for the day, or identify the most important thing for the day, or try to articulate something with which I'm struggling. Sometimes, I give myself a pep talk.

For example, here are a few recent entries... these are unedited, just the way I wrote them in my Goalpost for this month:

> 3/1: Oh, how I love the first of the month and what feels like a blank slate! I gained a couple of pounds last month, better up my walking and watch the snacking. I need to have a big Friday today,

a day of checking things off the list. But while I'm at it, maybe I can find a few things that are MORK.

3/3: The question of the day is what skills do I want to develop over the next three years? What will help me get where I want to be personally and professionally? Writing? What skills will help me be the best leader I can possibly be? Improve my public speaking? Get better at "networking"—I hate that word.

3/4: obsessing a bit about the 3Fs of skill development. How do I work that into what I'm doing? What if each month I add "skill development" to my monthly goal list?

3/6: feeling frustrated that I'm not getting enough done.... Like really not enough. So. Get organized. Set priorities. Knock them off in 50-minute blocks. GO.

3/7 Remembering that adventure is good, and considering how to get more adventure in my life. I think I should block 50 minutes today to begin planning an adventure.

3/8: Feeling defeated. Struggling not to catastrophize. Okay so that means that the best thing I can do today is focus on: 1) creating good content and 2) working on improving the product. The sun is shining, so getting my walk in is a must.

At the start of next month, I will reflect on how I performed against last month's goals and create a new goal list specifically for the month. I will once again enjoy the feeling of a "fresh slate" and begin, again, to track my progress and capture my thoughts along the way.

Now, this might seem like a whole lotta work, but truthfully, once the groundwork is laid, it is just a couple of minutes most days to be sure that I am living the life that I most want to lead. We all have goals; we all have dreams. And creating your own Goalpost is the most effective way I have ever found to be sure that you focus on what's important, recover when you fumble, and keep moving forward.

On today's walk, consider what current goals you are working toward. Can you clearly identify five to ten goals that you are actively working toward? When you get back, find a notebook or a few sheets of paper, write those goals down and start developing your own Goalpost notebook.

● ● ●

Walk # 42: Your Other Notebook

Ten years ago, Eric and I had an informal meeting with a guy named Steve who had created and sold an internet business before the tech bubble burst. Though details are not public, word on the street is that he sold his company for $40 million dollars. At the time of our meeting, he was retired at 35 and raising a couple of kids in the Hamptons. An introduction by a mutual friend led to a casual cup of coffee at our local coffee shop. The three of us sat down, ordered, and Steve took out a small, well-worn notebook and pen. Throughout our conversation, he made notes about anything that sparked his interest. Now, this is a guy who didn't need anything from us. He wasn't considering investing in our business or doing any kind of project together. Many people in his shoes would think *I've made my millions; I don't have anything to learn today*. But not Steve. He looked for every opportunity to discover something new and didn't miss an opportunity to capture a note of it.

I know I've mentioned my sister, who is one of the leading jewelry design consultants in the world and one of the most creative people I know. For as long as I can remember—literally for decades—she is never without a black and white speckled composition notebook into which goes every idea that she has, notes of people she's met, color combinations to try, articles she's cut out of magazines, and pretty much anything else that inspires her.

It's no surprise that note-taking is a habit of many of the world's most successful people. It accomplishes three things:

First, it captures things you hope to remember or need to finish and gets it out of your head and down on paper. That way you don't have to continue to work to try to remember the fact, the information, or the task—you know that it is safely captured for future reference.

Second, writing a note down helps you to memorize it because it forces you to process the information into your words and engages different parts of your brain, which helps to encode the information.

Third, note taking helps you filter. Sometimes something crosses your radar that you feel might be important or you have a good idea that you want to be sure to remember. Writing these things down and looking at them a few days later helps you sort the good ideas from the not-so-good ideas.

With our phones as our constant companions, there are many, many notetaking apps out there. I use a "to do" list app where I capture tasks that I need to complete, but I use an old-fashioned notebook and pen for more thoughtful things, such as drafting articles and making notes about something interesting someone said or something I've read.

I'm incredibly finicky about the notebooks I use. They must be spiral bound and small enough to fit in my tote bag, but big enough that I can write first drafts of articles. Not too expensive, since I go through them pretty quickly. And I love them. It's important to love your notebooks.

If you do not yet have a habit of capturing notes, goals, and dreams in a notebook, today is the day to begin to develop that habit.

After today's walk, find a notebook you love and a pen that writes smoothly and capture a thought, note, or idea. Then put that notebook in your bag and begin carrying it with you.

● ● ●

Walk # 43: Got a Problem?

Our business was in trouble. The changing digital media landscape had caused advertisers to look for new ways to reach their audience and those ways didn't exactly include what we were offering. So, as companies like ours were growing to reach more and more and more families, clients demanded more and more for less and less.

We had a problem. We had hundreds of people counting on us every day. I spent many nights losing sleep, fretting, and looking backward at all of the choices and decisions I had made in my life that brought me here to this moment. Yup, in the middle of the night, even I watch the replays and second-guess my choices.

None of this fretting, hand ringing, or worrying ever helps. Not one second spent second-guessing every decision I made since college graduation will ever help me solve a problem.

While everyone's problems are different, we all have challenges, things that are broken and things that we want to change in our lives. When you are caught in a problem, it is easy to let your mind travel down long, winding, and unproductive paths.

There's the catastrophe path that we talked about in Walk #38. At 2:00 a.m., I can easily walk that path and convince myself that my current challenges will ultimately lead to the loss of my home and my kids not being able to afford college.

There's the "where would I be if I had only..." path where I revisit all of the choices I've made and consider how different—and better—my life would be at this moment, had I made different choices.

There's the "I suck" path, where I simply loop through all of the mistakes I've made, the things I said that I shouldn't have, and the things I should have said that I didn't. The chocolate cake I ate. All the times I yelled at my kids.

Wouldn't it be better if we had a framework we could use to work through our challenges in a deliberate, thoughtful, and constructive way?

There are many problem-solving matrices out there. Here's mine. One caveat. Working through these ten steps doesn't guarantee you will come to the perfect solution. Sometimes your first solution will not be the right one. Sometimes, the correct solution will take time to implement. But if you continue to work through these specific problem-solving steps, you are less likely to burn critical mental energy on "what if," "I should have," or "I suck."

Step One: Figure out exactly what the problem is. Sometimes, what seems like the problem might not be the problem. Try to get to the root of it, not just the symptoms. Treat the problem like an onion and pull back layers. Ask questions of anyone who might have insight and do research to help you understand the problem better. Write down what you believe the problem is, then write down two other things that could be the problem.

Step Two: I love this one. Decide if the problem is really, truly yours. Is there someone else better positioned to solve it? Is it something you need to solve at all? This comes up very often when issues arise with my kids. My instinct as a mom is to try to fix every problem for them. But, sometimes the problem is theirs alone to solve.

Step Three: Take a moment to figure out if there are people who might be able to help you solve the problem. As women, we are often reluctant to ask for help, but chances are, if you have a problem, someone else has encountered it before. Consider asking for advice.

Step Four: Brainstorm as many different ways as you can to potentially solve the problem. Go big here. Think out of the box and consider "crazy" ideas, practical ideas—any and all ideas. Write them down. Don't edit, just aim to capture as many possible solutions as possible, regardless of how practical or impractical they might seem.

Step Five: Sometimes it helps to put the list away between step four and step five, but now you are going to go through your list of potential solutions, cross out the ones that don't make sense or you don't think will work and narrow it down to the best three or four. Keep an open mind when you do this because reviewing your list might possibly give rise to additional ideas.

Step Six: Evaluate the pros, cons, feasibility, and potential downsides or consequences of each of your remaining three or four ideas.

Step Seven: Choose one. Knowing it is a risk. Knowing you might choose wrong. Knowing that there is no guarantee of success. But place your bet and decide which course of action you are going to take.

Step Eight: Do the work. Implement the potential solution you have chosen 100%. Don't hedge. Don't go half in. Go all in and give that potential solution your 110% best effort.

Step Nine: Step back and evaluate if the plan has solved the problem. Be objective. Have you solved the problem? Improved the problem? Or, gulp, made the problem worse?

Step Ten: If you have solved the problem, congratulate yourself and cross it off your to-do list. If you have not solved the problem, don't panic. Simply go back to step one and try again.

Nope, this process will not instantly solve all of your problems. But through practice, you can train yourself to approach challenges in a more deliberate way.

How did it work for us? Well, the problem was the changing and evolving digital landscape and that was a problem beyond our control. But we had something no one else did: we had more than 500 moms who were deeply committed to the communities in which they lived. We had "boots on the ground" who could take digital into the real world. They could give product samples to friends and neighbors, host events and parties, and bring local moms into local stores. So that's what we did.

On today's walk, think about a problem you are wrestling with right now and brainstorm as many potential solutions as possible. Then, you get back, work through the problem-solving steps, and see where it leads you.

Walk # 44: Get Comfortable Being Uncomfortable

Ah, routines. How we love them. Taking the same route each day, engaging with the same people, listening to the same news shows, eating the same foods, and doing the same things. We are wired for consistency. We seek habits because they are safe and comfortable.

In *High-Performance Habits,* Brendon Burchard shares research that suggests that courage is a key to success. Courage, he explains, sometimes means simply taking "a first step toward real change in an unpredictable world."

Courage means taking action when the outcome is uncertain—when there is the risk of failure. It means stepping outside of the safe and predictable, taking a chance, and doing something different. Putting something on the line, even if what you are putting on the line is just your own internal sense of stability or security.

There's a lot of chatter about doing things that scare you and how you ought to face your fears. Oftentimes there is sage value to that conversation. But there is also a whole world of opportunity between things that scare you and things that push you outside of your comfort zone.

When my daughter was twelve, the thing that made her most uncomfortable was taking social risks. She was a kind, quiet, and likable kid who was struggling to understand the shifting dynamics of middle school. Her approach was to step back, let things play out, and avoid drama. A great plan in my opinion. But it also meant that she spent many weekends alone, waiting for her phone to buzz with an invitation. She was rarely the one to initiate plans.

One day, she was listlessly hanging around the house on a Saturday afternoon. "Text a friend," I suggested, as I often did.

"Nah," she said noncommittedly.

Eric overheard the conversation, playing out for probably the hundredth time between us.

"You know," he said, "to get what you want, sometimes you need to get comfortable being uncomfortable."

She looked at him and you could see the wheels turning. She wandered off in that nonchalant way of a teenager and came back twenty minutes later. "Can you give me a ride to town?" she asked. "I'm meeting Lucy."

And for the coming year, that became our family mantra: get comfortable being uncomfortable.

In order to make changes in your life, you don't need to constantly take tremendous risks or show huge leaps of courage—though sometimes big leaps and huge courage is called for. But meaningful change can come as the result of pushing just outside your comfort zone. Being willing to put yourself in situations which are unfamiliar, unexpected, or uncertain.

Here are some examples of things that make me uncomfortable, but I regularly do them anyway. Flying—for someone who travels as much as I do, it is shocking how uncomfortable flying makes me. Conflict—I hate having difficult conversations. Going to a new gym—I'm always afraid I will embarrass myself or that I will do something stupid and get hurt.

On today's walk, consider some of the things that make you uncomfortable. New people? New places? New foods? Difficult conversations? Note what puts that tight feeling of fear in your belly. Things that make you uncomfortable. Consider whether those things really put you at risk or simply are things that, well, make you uncomfortable. When you get back, make a list of three things that make you uncomfortable that are holding you back from living the life you want to live. Then, make the conscious decision to work toward being comfortable being uncomfortable.

● ● ●

Walk # 45: This Too Shall Pass

When I was 26 and recently divorced from a disastrous "starter marriage" (that I'd entered into at barely 23), I remember saying—often—"It is a world of possibilities." I felt that in my gut as I walked into my office, wearing a beautiful suit, greeting the receptionist, and asking how her weekend was, cranking out a perfectly-crafted brief, or speaking up in a meeting with the general counsel of Revlon and having his assistant send a huge bag of cosmetic samples to my office later that day. I felt that as I left the office at 6:15 on Thursday evenings to take a screenwriting class, even though every other lawyer was staying until at least 8:00. I felt that way when I went to the gym and grew stronger each day. And I felt that way when I walked away from that job to pursue my dreams of writing, living by the beach, and, ultimately, a new wonderful marriage and entrepreneurship. It was a world of possibilities.

As I laid in bed some twenty years later, I felt defeated. Dreams I envisioned at 26 hadn't come true. Yet others I had never imagined were all around me: a home, husband, kids, and dog I loved. A community I cherished. The ability to ski a black diamond from the top of a mountain in Colorado. Not to mention a business that gives me the opportunity to connect with, encourage, and inspire hundreds of women.

It wasn't enough. I never wrote the book. I reached, inspired, and supported hundreds of women—not thousands. In short, I hadn't changed the world.

Yet.

One of my greatest personal challenges is the defeated feeling that wherever I am is where I will stay. If things are hard, I "know" that they will always be hard. If my job is awful, it will never change. If I hurt my back, I will always be in pain. If my daughter is sad, she will be sad forever. If my dog is making me crazy, he will always get me up in the middle of the night to go out, always bark like a lunatic when someone walks past my house, and always throw up when he sees us pull out the suitcases for a trip.

For as long as I can remember, my mother would say "this too shall pass." It is a phrase that traces its roots back hundreds of years that found its way into Jewish folklore and a speech by Abraham Lincoln. Though I don't know for sure, I suspect it is a phrase my mother inherited from her mother.

"This too shall pass."

When I was younger, as with most things my mother said, the phrase annoyed me (fortunately, I've outgrown this tendency). "You don't understand," I would think. "This sucks, and I don't see a way out." But as with many pieces of maternal advice, I have come to appreciate this phrase more and more.

At some point, the challenges we face in a given moment will disappear. You have two choices. You can spend your time and mental energy bemoaning the tough space you are in right now and feel stuck. Or you can embrace the struggle for the gifts it gives you, be grateful for the lessons that struggle is trying to teach you, and do the work you need to do to move past it.

What you don't need to do is lie in bed and think about how much the current struggle sucks.

On today's walk, let's think about the places in our lives where we feel stuck and remind ourselves that, whether by our own hand, or by the sheer passage of time, things will change. Challenging toddlers will become challenging teenagers who will one day head out into the world on their own. Impossible bosses will quit or get fired. Dogs we love, despite their sometimes obnoxious behavior, will cross the rainbow bridge.

This too shall pass.

Remembering that opens the door to two valuable things.

First, we can choose to focus on the good in the challenge. We can appreciate how smart, loyal, and fun that otherwise challenging dog is. We can learn the lessons to be learned from that bad boss.

Second, we can push past the feeling of defeat that often accompanies feeling stuck, embrace the struggle and do the work that will help us move past it.

On today's walk, think about a place in your life where you feel stuck. Take a deep breath and remind yourself that, whatever it is, it will change. Consider what work you need to do to get unstuck and commit to working for change.

Walk # 46: Grit is Hard

I'm a sprinter, not a marathoner. I love nothing more than to explore a new idea, develop a new skill, or dig into a new project. I love to learn new things, solve puzzles, and figure things out.

When I was a kid, I approached the start of each school semester with a feeling of excitement and new beginnings. I loved the clean slate that a pile of brightly colored, empty notebooks represented. The promise of new teachers and new ideas. The chance to start again.

As a litigator, my work followed a similar pattern. A new case would come in, presenting an entirely new story and new cast of characters. Often, there was a new business or industry to learn and new people to get to know. I would dig in, feeling excited and inspired. The first time I represented an advertising agency, I went straight to the bookstore and bought a book on the history of the advertising industry (it was before you could rely on the internet for that kind of background). During my fifteen-year career, I learned about the insurance industry, the pharmaceutical industry, the media industry, the beauty industry, and the way organized crime controlled the concrete business in New York in the 1980s.

I loved getting started. But then the grind would begin. Interrogatories, pleadings, discovery motions, and boxes—sometimes thousands of boxes—of documents. Hearings, research, depositions, and arguments with opposing counsel. The cases I worked on would drag on for years.

Inevitably, they would end—either with a settlement worked out when one side had finally had enough or with a judge's ruling—and there would come a day when suddenly a case that had consumed my life for years would disappear. I remember the relief of packing up all of the documents from my office, labeling them carefully, and sending them off to storage. And then the cycle would start again.

It is the middle part of any journey toward an important goal that is tricky. The first few days of a new commitment to changing your diet and losing weight? Easy. The months of commitment that it takes to bring about real change? Hard. Deciding to write a book and sitting down to write the first thirty pages? Easy. So easy in fact, that I've done it a dozen times.

But now is when it gets hard. Now is when it gets tedious. Now is when the voices in my head begin their barrage of questions and doubt: *Is it good enough? Is it a waste of time? No one is going to want to read this.* Yet, the book you are holding in your hands exists only because I pushed through the voices in my head.

The middle is when the work comes, when you need to dig deep and find the grit to keep going. The middle is when it's not fun.

What happens if you push through the tedium and do the work? What is on the other side? Angela Duckworth, who is often credited with coining the word "grit" and identifying its importance to success, defines grit in this way:

Grit is passion and perseverance for long-term and meaningful goals.

For many of us, passion is easy, but perseverance is hard. These three things are your most likely obstacles:

1. The voices in your head
2. The tedium of the project
3. Life

On today's walk, think about something in your life that you've wanted to accomplish, something that you've started and then quit. Ask yourself how important it is to you. If it is something you've started over and over, chances are it is pretty important.

Now picture yourself doing the work needed to accomplish that goal. Really picture it. What does that look like day in and day out? Accept the fact that it will be hard and tedious and sometimes boring. Know that, at some point, the voices in your head will tell you that you are wasting your time or are likely, once again, to fail. Decide that you are going to ignore those voices and push through. Lastly, know that life gets in the way. That's why it's called life. You will eat a giant piece of birthday cake, skip three walks in a row because of bad weather, and stare at a blank computer screen and feel you have nothing of value to say.

Simply knowing that these challenges are coming can, in and of itself, help you press through. Look at these obstacles mindfully and objectively, then get up again and do the work.

●●●

Walk # 47: Seriously, It Can't Be This Easy

Want to be happier? Learn to see the cup half full, rather than half empty. Count your blessings. Appreciate the positive. Retrain your brain to focus on the good. And for heaven's sake, stop worrying.

Sounds easy right?

In a sense, it is. Oodles of research has shown that being grateful unlocks an almost magical path to happiness. In a well-documented research study titled *Counting Blessings Versus Burdens: An Experimental Investigation of Gratitude and Subjective Well-Being in Daily Life*, professors Robert A. Emmons and Michael E. McCullough found that the participants who focused on the things for which they were grateful were happier, exercised more, and made greater progress toward their goals than those who did not.

So why don't we just... well, why don't we just do that?

First, we are hard-wired to identify risks. If our ancient ancestors chose to wander into the sunshine, appreciating the warmth on their face and not considering the saber-toothed tiger stalking them from the woods, well, you can imagine how that could end. Recognizing danger and remaining vigilant of risk has been critical to our survival as a species. As we've discussed before, we are hard-wired with a negativity bias.

Second, we are superstitious. I was traveling to Europe with a friend who is afraid to fly. As we boarded, she patted the outside of the plane, much the way you would pat a beloved child on the head. Once onboard, she peeked into the cockpit and introduced herself to the pilot. Minutes later, as the plane took off, she closed her eyes and furrowed her brow.

"Are you okay?" I asked.

"Yes. I'm trying to keep the plane in the air with my mind," she replied.

We believe that we can keep bad things from happening if we follow our routines, rub our rabbit's feet, or think really, really hard about them. We are afraid to "tempt fate" by counting our blessings or making changes.

Third, media feeds us a constant stream of negative news and stories. In fact, some estimates show that 90% of the news we are shown is negative. Watch the news, listen to the radio, or read a newsfeed online and it would be reasonable to believe that nothing good happens in the world.

Finally, as people, we are always striving for forward movement: the next promotion or the bigger house. We want our kids to bring home better grades, our salaries to be bigger, and pretty much every single one of us wants to be thinner, stronger, taller—something-er.

That is not a bad thing. But it is tricky to be grateful for what you have while simultaneously striving for more. On some level, we are afraid that if we are really, truly, deeply appreciative of what we have right now, it will tamp down our ambition and our drive. We fear that by thinking *Wow, where I am right now is awesome. I love my house and my partner and my kids and everything is great*—we will settle. The kids will keep fighting, your husband will continue to leave his laundry in the middle of the floor, and you will never lose the extra twenty pounds of "baby weight" you're still carrying around. For those of us with type-A tendencies and big dreams, practicing gratefulness can feel like a recipe for settling.

Despite all of this, it is possible to retrain your brain to focus on the positive and literally change the way you navigate the world on a day to day, real-life basis.

Ready for the secret?

Focus on the positive and be grateful.

Yup, learning to be more grateful—and therefore learning to be happier—is largely a function of just doing it. The more you do it, the more you create the habit of looking at the glass half full and begin to retrain your brain to create new pathways to gratefulness.

How?

The simplest way—that research shows is very effective—is simply to maintain a gratitude journal in which you record something for which you are grateful for every day. There is no one right way to do this: you can go old school and use any kind of notebook, buy a printed "gratitude journal" with daily prompts, start a new note on your phone, or download one of the many gratitude journal apps.

But here's the key. There is only one thing that will make this work. The part that is hard. For this to have an impact, for this practice to really begin to change your neural pathways and begin to make you happier, you must do this every day. For months. Better yet, forever.

If you are not serious about making the commitment to becoming more grateful, more appreciative and happier, the prettiest new gratitude journal or most intuitive app will not make a difference.

But if you want to change the way you perceive the world in a manner that compelling research shows is pretty much guaranteed to make you happier, start writing down one thing you are grateful for and do it every single day.

Starting today.

On today's walk, mentally list as many things as you can think of for which you are grateful. Big things, sure, but don't forget the small things. The tiny things. The sneakers you love and the legs that carry you forward. Your health. The coffee waiting for you at the end of your walk. Anything and everything.

Walk # 48: You Control the Input

On our last walk, we talked briefly about how much of the news we consume is negative—90% by some estimates. Ever notice how they always leave the feel-good story for the last thirty-seconds? On today's walk, let's think about how much control we have over the input we let in.

When Mason was barely two, Eric and I inadvertently saw three movies in a row in which a child died. It hadn't been something we chose to do deliberately—we hadn't researched the movies before we went to see them. We just took what we heard from friends or online. "Oh, yes, see *Pay it Forward*, it was excellent," and avoided spoiler alerts. Never again, we vowed. To this day, we will turn off any television program and avoid any movie where a child dies.

During the last election cycle, we watched a whole lot of political coverage and we watched it descend from "here is this politician's stand on this important issue" to name-calling and bullying, with politicians and pundits treating one another in ways that we wouldn't allow our children to behave on the playground. No more. Yes, I want to understand the facts and the implications of a politician's position on issues I care about, but I had to turn off the anger and brutality.

When social media was in its infancy, I often found myself being pulled into all kinds of content. The chance to read a stranger's personal, unfiltered thoughts or peek into their lives was fascinating. But too often I let that turn into a two-hour round of compare and despair. Now, I use social media to keep in touch with people I care about and that is all. Well, pretty much all.

And finally, there are the friends and people in my life who thrive on negativity and gossip, who never miss an opportunity to put someone else down, criticize their husband, or complain about their children. Little by little, I have reduced the time I spend with them.

In our multimedia, multiplatform, constantly connected world, a startling amount of news, stories, blog posts, videos and social media ranting is available. Every day. All the time. While some of that input is positive, much of it is negative. We control what content we allow in on a daily basis.

We choose the television shows we watch, what news stories we read, and who we spend time with.

This is not about denial. Tragic things happen every day. And that is kind of the point. Sad things happen in the real world and must be felt, experienced, and dealt with. You do not need to add dramatized, fiction-alized tragedies to your life. You do not need friends who feed you gossip and thrive on other people's misery.

I'm not suggesting that you tune out every piece of negative informa-tion and encase yourself in a bubble of false positivity.

First, sometimes there are lessons to be learned about grief or trag-edy. For instance, while I refuse to watch any movie or television show in which a child dies for boosted ratings, I read—and loved—every word of *The Angel in My Pocket*, a memoir by Sukey Forbes about her experience after the death of her daughter. The difference? For me, *The Angel in my Pocket* was so deeply authentic and powerfully written, and was clearly *not* written for the sake of shock value or to sell books, but rather to share the author's story in a way that was compelling and important.

Second, to live fully in this world means you need to know what is go-ing on around you, both locally and in the broader context. The human toll of war and famine and tsunamis should be faced and acknowledged by all of us because, as part of the global human community, we can all have a hand in making the world a better place and the only way to do that is if you know what the heck is going on in the world.

But there is a difference between being informed and educated and watching an endless loop of tragic television. If you want to live the very best life you can, you need stories that empower you. That inspire you. That fire you up for success. Be it *Rocky, G.I. Jane, Field of Dreams, Hairspray,* or *Miracle on 34th Street,* fill your mind with stories of suc-cess, power, beauty or entertainment that make you want to get up and dance. So, the next time you find yourself getting sucked into this week's *Dateline* tragedy, just say NO. Remember: you control the input.

On today's walk, think about the inputs you allow in during the course of a typical day. What stories do you read, what conversations do you have, what radio do you listen to, what television do you watch? How does each make you feel? What input gives you real value of information and education and what input depletes your energy and makes you sad or angry? Are you balancing the input?

Walk # 49: A Tale of Two Marshmallows

After the incident with the yellow scale that forced me to face the reality of a forty-six-pound weight gain in the winter of my sophomore year of college, I returned to school a week later and began an eight-month journey to get my body back.

What in the world does this have to do with marshmallows?

One of the tactics that I employed during those long eight months was the following. If I was craving something junky—be it pizza or ice cream or whatever was not part of my plan to rid myself of that extra forty-six pounds—I would make a deal with myself: If I still wanted it the next day, I would eat it. Sometimes I did, but more often than not, the next day would come and go and I would forget how desperately I had wanted that vanilla swirl ice cream cone.

While this was only part of my informal weight loss plan, it was a key element in my ultimate success. It took me eight months to get back to my pre-college weight and though there was more to it—lots of walking, no more nighttime pizza, no second helpings—I recall my willingness to both delay gratification of something I wanted and forgive myself when I ate the Snickers bar the next day as key elements of my success.

There may be more to this willingness and ability to delay gratification. In the late 1960s, a researcher from Stanford University began a series of experiments that have become known as the Marshmallow Study. The premise was fairly simple. A group of young kids (mostly ages four and five) were invited into a room and offered two choices: they could enjoy a single marshmallow treat right away, or they could wait fifteen minutes—with the marshmallow right in front of them—and if they were able to refrain from eating the marshmallow for fifteen minutes, they were given two marshmallows to eat. Denying temptation and delaying gratification for fifteen minutes gave them twice the reward.

Most of the kids fidgeted, struggling to fight temptation and gave in at some point before the fifteen minutes were up. But some kids were able to hold fast, knowing that if they held on just a bit longer, the reward would be worth it. And here's where it got interesting.

The researchers followed these children into their teens and adulthood and discovered that the children who were able to delay gratification, who had the fortitude to resist immediate satisfaction for a "bigger pay-off," performed better than the kids who gave into immediate gratification. They performed better on their SATs, earned more money, reported greater levels of happiness, showed lower levels of depression, and maintained healthier weights throughout their lives.

Now, the Marshmallow Test is only part of the puzzle, as the researchers didn't explore the underlying factors of the children's experiences or personalities that enabled some to delay gratification and made others unable to resist. Undoubtedly, there were other factors at play here.

But one thing is clear. The ability, or willingness, to make choices *now* that will lead to your success *then*, is a critical element of your ability to succeed in achieving whatever goals you have set for yourself. I call it "playing the long game"—understanding that what you do today will cause the results you see tomorrow. Keep in mind that sometimes you do need to eat the chocolate swirl ice cream cone.

While there is a lot of experience and psychology underlying an individual's ability to delay gratification in favor of something you want more, it is a skill that can be nurtured. How you put this into practice in your own life depends on what your goals are and what you are doing that doesn't align with those goals. But being aware of the choices you make, pausing to ask yourself if the choice you are making now aligns with your more important future goals, and being forgiving when you sometimes (emphasis on sometimes) decide that the satisfaction is worth it are the first steps.

On today's walk, consider your goals and make a deal with yourself: Next time you want to do something that doesn't align with your goals, you will wait. If you still want to spend thirty minutes on social media after you've read five pages of a book that has the potential to make your life better, you will. And if you still want that ice cream cone tomorrow, go for it. But order a small.

Walk # 50: People Are Like Bananas

My daughter likes her bananas green. Once they turn yellow, she declares them mushy and inedible. She shares this preference with my dad, who also likes his bananas more green than yellow. My son and I both prefer our bananas fully ripe and yellow. This means that when we go to the grocery store, we are likely to buy two different bunches of bananas—one green and one yellow. Now here's the tricky part: we have one large, beautiful wooden fruit bowl that sits on our counter, typically filled with apples, oranges, nectarines, and, of course, bananas. But if we put both bunches of bananas in the fruit bowl next to each other, my daughter's green bananas quickly turn yellow.

Why? Apparently, bananas give off a compound called ethylene that encourages their underripe neighbors to catch up fast. As a result, bananas in a bunch achieve an equal level of ripeness at the same time.

Like bananas, research shows that you are very likely to resemble the people in your bunch. You are likely to hold many of the same beliefs, achieve similar levels of financial and professional success, and share similar characteristics of weight and wellness. If your friends are happier, you are likely to be happier.

Jim Rohn famously suggested, "You are the average of the five people you spend the most time with." Although research suggests it is not that simple, there can be no doubt that the people with whom you surround yourself have a profound influence on your life. That means that you can accelerate your growth and accomplishments by changing your social circles and spending time with people who embody the life to which you aspire.

Of course, in practicality, this is not so easy. If you want to be a millionaire, it might not be practical to find five millionaires to suddenly become your besties. And there are countless stories of super successful people who have achieved great things despite less than optimal surroundings and circumstances.

But it does suggest that making some shifts in how you spend your time and who you spend it with can impact your ability to live the life you want.

Let's consider happiness. If each day you drop your kids at school and meet a group of four other moms for coffee who spend that coffee hour complaining about their lives, chances are you will join in that conversation and focus your attention on all of the negatives in your own life.

Conversely, if your morning coffee group is comprised of a group of positive people who focus on gratitude and bring hope and enthusiasm for the day ahead, you are likely to leave your morning coffee feeling hopeful and enthusiastic.

Staying with the coffee example... if the group with whom you have morning coffee tend to start their day with donuts, you are highly likely to follow suit. Conversely, if your crew opts instead to start their day with an egg white omelet, you are likely to adopt a similar habit.

So, what does this mean? Does this mean we should drop our old friends because they don't "measure up" to our ideal or don't share our goals and ambition?

No. More recent research suggests that you are not simply the average of the five people with whom you spend the most time. Rather, all of the people in your social circle have influence. So, you don't have to "drop" your closest friends. Rather, you can expand your circle to bring in new people and new ideas.

If your morning coffee crew orders donuts every morning and kicks off the day with a flood of negativity, perhaps you take one or two days a week to skip morning coffee and take a walk. Who knows, maybe you will be the ripe banana that encourages them to join you.

On today's walk, think about the people with whom you spend the most time. Do their values, habits, and goals align with yours? If not, consider expanding your circle.

● ● ●

Walk # 51: Move Your Beach Chair Back

On our last walk, we talked about the value of expanding your social circle to include people who can bring new things to your life. One way to do that is to move your beach chair back.

Living just a few miles from the beach, on summer nights we often gather an ad hoc group of friends to meet at the beach for an informal "beach party." These are rarely planned more than a day or two in advance and, more often than not, are planned—if you could even call it planning—the day of.

Everyone brings something to contribute—often whatever leftovers were in their fridge. Within an hour, the two big folding tables would be overloaded with all kinds of food, from noodle salad to thinly sliced steak and an occasional pizza. A circle of chairs would be set up around a hole that had been dug for the bonfire that would be lit after the sunset. More people would show up, place their bowls on the table, pour a glass of wine or open a beer and bring their chairs over. Those of us who had already been sitting around the future fire would stand up and drag our chairs back a bit further to make more room, extending the circle.

These beach parties would go on for hours and always included a varied group of people. Houseguests who were out for the weekend would come. Kevin would have to go to work at the restaurant he managed, but his wife Kelly would stay late into the night with their two kids. New neighbors were invited and welcomed into the fold. All told, these beach parties ranged from eight people to up to forty and occasionally more.

There was magic to these beach parties. People began with awkward introductions. A glass of wine would be poured into a paper cup. "Are you local?" was often the first question asked, or in other words, Hamptons code for, *"Do you actually live here and send your kids to our schools or are you a 'city person' out for the weekend?"* Conversations deepened as the sun set.

But it was the kids I always watched with awe. Kids of varied ages, many of whom didn't know each other before the evening's gathering. For some reason, at the beach, parents tended not to do much to get their kids engaged. They don't seem to worry much. We were at the beach, after all, and there was plenty of food to be had just sitting on the table. There were sandcastles to build, holes to be dug, and lifeguard stands to climb. The parents, even those who were generally accustomed to carefully managing their kids' lives, seemed to be willing to tell their kids, "You're at the beach, go figure it out."

And the kids did. Within an hour, no matter the age, gender, or friendships that had existed before that night, a pack of kids would form. Running and playing together. Digging holes, playing tag, and letting the waves chase their toes at the edge of the water. They would run for hours, laughing. A whole pack of kids.

At some point, bags of marshmallows were fished out, and the kids returned to the bonfire—sticks in hand—and settled in beside their parents to roast marshmallows. Invariably, a good-natured debate would arise over the merits of marshmallows that were meticulously toasted to a light brown color versus those that were charred black on the outside and gooey on the inside. Constellations were considered and shooting stars searched for.

These were magical nights that taught me three things.

First, there is always room to move your chairs out and extend the circle.

Second, given the right set of circumstances, children will make their own fun.

Third, being in nature brings out the best in people.

On today's walk, think about your community and the circle you create around your metaphorical bonfire. Can you move your chairs out and extend your circle? Can you create an environment where your kids can run like a pack of kids?

Walk # 52: Frogs First

Next to my desk is a wooden tray—an old-fashioned "inbox." In it is usually a random pile of papers that need attention—bills to be paid, forms to be filled out. I suspect you have a similar pile someplace in your life. Some of the tasks in that inbox are simple and take only a moment to do, like filling out the permission slip for my daughter's field trip to the aquarium or paying the $28 water bill. Others are far more complicated, overwhelming, or frightening, like the unopened bill from a recent sonogram of the lump behind my ear (it turned out to be nothing, but the cost was not covered by insurance). The letter from the Federal Trademark office that it is time to renew our company's trademark. The incomplete draft of my will.

Often, I begin with the things I want to do and put off some of the things that I need to do. The hard things. The challenging things. But mostly, I put off the scary things or the things I don't want to face. The unopened medical bill and that will.

Most of us procrastinate doing the things we don't want to do. And why not? There is plenty to do each and every day and we can easily fill our day doing the things we enjoy, and to an extent, that's okay—we shouldn't sacrifice what we enjoy for what we don't enjoy.

But some of those procrastinations must be completed. The bill from that sonogram must be paid. The trademark renewal must be filed. The garbage must be taken out, bills must be paid, and a decision must be made about the kids' guardians so that the will can be completed.

Procrastination is bad because when you put off the tasks you don't enjoy but must get done, they tend to grow bigger and bigger and harder and harder. Each and every time you think about them and choose not to get them done, you have expended mental energy on the task, but have not accomplished a thing.

Years ago, I read a book on personal productivity titled *Eat that Frog* by Brian Tracy. While I don't remember much of the book, I do remember this central theme: if you have five things to eat and one of them is a frog, wouldn't you eat the frog first to get it over with? Then, you can move on to the ice cream sundae.

Though I hope that there are no frogs on your menu, the moral of the story is a good one. Each day, identify the task that you are dreading and DO IT FIRST. Yes, I know it is counterintuitive. Who wants to do what's dreaded the most when you can do the more joyful things? But we all have things that we must do and don't enjoy. We have work tasks that we push to the bottom of the pile over and over. For some, it's sales calls. For others, it's chasing down those overdue invoices. Writer's block? Yup, that too.

On today's walk, think about a few of the things that are on your to-do list that you have been pushing to the bottom of the pile, either practically (that hospital bill) or mentally (calling your sister to clear the air from your argument last Easter). Then, when you get back from today's walk, do one of those things. Today. Before you do anything else.

Join me in an experiment. Starting tomorrow, and for seven straight days, begin each day by identifying the frog on your to-do list. Move it to the front of the line. Do it first. Then be mindful of how the rest of the day goes. Are you a bit more productive? A little more relaxed? Do you feel a significant sense of accomplishment or relief? Were the joyful tasks that much more fun?

Walk # 53: Don't Be a Jelly Donut

One of the first businesses Eric and I launched was a pet product business. We manufactured dog treats, cat treats, and horse treats. Everything we produced was human grade and manufactured in bakeries that otherwise made only human food. We used to snack regularly on the allergy-free dog treats—baked treats that used tapioca flour and banana. They were delicious.

At some point, we outgrew the small local bakery that made our dog treats and were interviewing larger commercial bakeries. At one such meeting, we were sitting in the office of the president of a larger commercial bakery when he shared with us some research that had been conducted by one of his clients—one of the country's largest cookie companies.

"They were trying to figure out the perfect balance of sugar and fat for the American palate," he explained. "So they conducted a series of focus groups and what they discovered was the higher they raised the fat and the higher they raised the sugar, the more people liked it. Basically, they couldn't raise the fat and sugar too high for the American consumer."

I was surprised, but not so surprised. I thought back to when I was about six years old and my best friend Jenny and I used to bake chocolate chip cookies in her kitchen. We would begin by mashing together butter and sugar with the back of a wooden spoon until it formed a paste. It was delicious. We could have stopped right there, and sometimes we did.

We are hard-wired to crave fat and sugar. That's just how it is. When all of those easy, readily available calories are available to you, your body wants as much as it can get because our ancestors didn't live in a world of abundance of food, they lived in a world of scarcity. So you better eat up when you can.

Not only are you hard-wired to want it, but study after study has shown that sugar is addictive. The more you eat, the more you want. One study suggests that sugar is more addictive than cocaine—at least in rats.

Bottom line: You want fat and sugar and once you have some, you want more.

And sugar is bad for you. Like, really bad. It increases your risk of diabetes and has been linked to increased risk of cancer, heart disease, and depression. It causes spikes in your blood sugar and leads to crashes in your energy. It negatively impacts your ability to concentrate, contributes to weight gain, and can contribute to migraines, acne, and joint pain.

Okay, so we crave it, it is addictive, and it is bad for us. What do we do?

Sorry, there's no easy answer. We have to start by accepting that the old adage is true: you are what you eat. The food you eat provides the building blocks for your entire body. Everything you put into your mouths becomes the fuel, fiber, muscles, and more that comprise the body in which you walk through life.

You can choose to be a jelly donut, with a body nourished by globs of strawberry jam, fat, and sugar crystals. Or you can choose to be carrots and hummus. It's up to you to decide what fuels your body.

On today's walk, think about what you choose to eat on a regular basis. How much sugar are you allowing into your body? How strong is your sugar addiction? Mentally walk through your day and think about what you typically eat and where the sugar is hiding. Decide that you are going to eat less sugar today.

● ● ●

Walk # 54: Sacrifice: How Much is Too Much?

I was driving alone with my son when he was about four and the subject turned to his favorite "Aunt Sue," a dear friend who was childless at the time. Out of the blue, my son said, "I hope Aunt Sue never has a baby."

"Why?" I asked, assuming the answer would be something along the lines of *"Because then she won't have as much time for me."* But that wasn't it at all. He said, "Because having kids is so hard, and I want Aunt Sue to be happy."

Yikes. What behavior was I modeling? What message was I sending? That being a mom was more work than joy?

Every parent makes sacrifices for her children. It starts with your waistline and, well, never ends. But how much sacrifice is too much? When did it become a badge of honor to sacrifice your entire self for your children?

We have created a society that discourages moms from taking care of themselves and applauds them for making a total sacrifice of self. Simultaneously, we are bombarded with messages about how perfect everything should look and feel.

It's so very wrong on so many levels.

First, you can't be everything for everyone unless you have first taken care of yourself. It's been said over and over in so very many ways. But how often do you listen? How often do you say *no* to one of your children's requests so that you can take a bubble bath? How often do you ask a friend/husband/mother/sister to watch your kids for an hour so you can take a walk? Ridiculous right? Sure, you'll ask for help if you need to take your father to the doctor, but asking someone to watch your kids so you can read a book? *Never*? As I thought. So... you will ask people for help so that you to take care of other people, but not to take care of yourself, right?

Second, you deserve it. I know, I know. Your kids need you. You have work to do. You're busy. But there is only one of you and I know how incredible you are. I know that you deserve the very best, most beautiful, incredible life that you can create. You deserve to wake up in the morning feeling good. You deserve to look in the mirror and like what you see. You deserve limber muscles, pretty toes, loyal friends and a long and healthy life.

Finally, we teach our children the wrong message with too much self-sacrifice. Do you want your kids to grow up believing that the complete surrender of self is the obligation of parenthood? Probably not. More likely what you wish for them is a life filled with love, joy, and, dare I say it, balance. The ability to have a family, but also to have interests, friends, faith, and love. If that is what you want for your children, then that is what you should model. See the paradox? If you want your children to have the best life they possibly can, then you must show them that it is possible to be a great parent and still take great care of yourself. You must teach them that it is okay for mom to sometimes put herself first. So, if you won't do it for yourself, do it for your kids.

On today's walk, give yourself the space to think about all the sacrifices you make for your family and decide for yourself if you are sacrificing too much. Are you depleted? Are you irritable? Are you snappy and impatient? Has your weight, fitness, or wellness suffered? Remind yourself that you deserve to have a happy, fulfilling life and that by taking the steps to be the best version of you, you will be modeling how to be the best version of them.

Walk # 55: A Different Kind of Exercise

"And, I've started meditating," the petite, hard-charging media exec with whom I was having lunch said. She had left her high profile, high stress, kind-of-job-you-read-about-in-business-magazines job as a media exec about nine months before and was taking, in her words, a gap year. At 50-something. Of course a gap year for a woman like Sharon includes three consulting projects, the launch of a new business, a trip to Asia, and, apparently, meditation.

"I've always wanted to meditate," I confided, "but I suck at it." And you see, right there is the obvious problem. Meditation is supposed to be non-judgmental. You are supposed to "accept" where you are. The fact that I believe I suck at meditating just points at exactly how much I, well, suck at meditating.

It's not that I haven't tried. One of my favorite places in my home is my closet. It is small, but it has a window and in the morning at just the right moment, the sun streams through that tiny window. When my kids were young, it was one of the few places they didn't look for me. Occasionally, I would go into the closet, sit cross-legged on the floor and try to take five deep, mindful breaths. Then I reduced my expectation (you see, I have high expectations, yet another reason I suck at meditating) to three mindful breaths.

"I started with an app," Sharon said sipping her—you guessed it—herbal tea.

"There are meditation apps?" I asked, which was probably a silly question. There are apps for everything, right? Yet, somehow meditation seemed to be something that should be technology-free. But maybe I had been going about this all wrong. Maybe my beloved technology could be the key to unlocking my inner peace. I listened closely as I took another slurp of my black coffee.

"There are several," Sharon said. "Why don't you try one on the bus home?" Sharon and I had met in midtown and I was staring at my usual two-hour commute back home later that afternoon.

And so I did. I selected one of the many meditation apps, downloaded it to my phone and, for ten minutes, listened as Andy Puddicombe, a Brit with a gentle voice and lovely accent, suggested that I focus on my breath. I promptly fell asleep and considered that a win.

Over the course of the next eighteen months, my relationship with meditation ebbed and flowed. I tested different apps. Tried again to take five slow, mindful breaths on the floor of my closet. Tried to practice "mindfulness" while brushing my teeth. Success came and went.

Until the day I changed my entire perspective on meditating.

I don't particularly like to do burpees, a hateful exercise where you drop to the floor on your belly and then somehow manage to spring up to standing and do a little jump. I hate dropping to the floor of the gym. I hate how incredibly awkward and ungraceful burpees are, at least when I do them. I hate lying on the dirty gym floor over and over. But mostly, I hate how hard they are.

I do them anyway. Because they are a great exercise that helps my entire body get stronger. Because practicing the action of getting up from the floor is one of those functional movements that I believe will continue to serve me as I age, and I plan to be one of those eighty-year-olds who can spring up from the floor.

I do burpees because they are a good form of exercise for my body.

Eventually, I also came to understand that meditation is a good—probably one of the best—forms of exercise for my brain. And when I'm that eighty-year-old who can still do burpees, I want my brain to be right there with me.

So, I committed to a daily meditation of ten minutes. Well, most days. I do it when I don't want to. I do it when I do it badly. I do it when it is the last thing I feel like doing.

Because here's the thing... If I only did burpees when I "felt like it" I would never do them. Mediation is simply a different form of exercise.

On today's walk, think about what kind of exercise you are doing to calm and focus your mind and consider making a commitment to exercising your brain the same way you exercise your body.

● ● ●

Walk # 56: Money Can Buy Happiness. Just Kidding. Sort of.

We've all heard it, over and over and over: money can't buy happiness. But, well, let's face it—rich people look happier. They look like they take more vacations and have more adventures. They look healthier. They dress better. They live in more beautiful homes and drive fancier cars. They have people to clean their homes and cook their meals. All in all, they look happier.

For those of us who struggle to figure out how to make our paychecks cover the bills each month, dread the mysterious rattle in our cars that suggests something bad is coming, and have no idea how we are going to help our kids pay for college—much less retire one day—well, it sure looks like money buys happiness. Or at least a sense of security that allows you to pursue happiness.

Over the past couple of decades, there has been a lot of research on happiness, including whether or not money buys happiness. Here's what they found.

If you do not have enough money to cover your basic necessities and to feel secure, then yup, more money is likely to help make you a bit happier. This means that if you are genuinely struggling every month, either more money in or less money out would likely make you a little happier.

However, once you have achieved a level where your income covers your essentials, more money is unlikely to have an impact on your happiness.

That's not to say that with more money you might dress better, take more vacations or drive a fancier car, it is just that the research has consistently shown that those things will not make you happier. I swear, it's true.

There appears to be several reasons why.

First, ultimately, *things* don't make people happy. You get used to your stuff and, once the initial thrill of buying something new and fancy is over, research shows that *stuff* doesn't make you happy. Let me repeat that: stuff does not make you happy.

Second, as you acquire more money, stuff, and stature, research shows that you will quickly adjust to your new level and once again want more. You will continue to move the goal line and continue to convince yourself that you will be happy when you hit that next level. But you won't.

Third, if you are looking at others who have more and engaging in "compare and despair" you will never have enough because there will always be someone who dresses better, takes more vacations, or drives a fancier car. Always.

Now that's not to say that striving is bad. Wanting more, dreaming big, and working hard is the stuff of a fulfilling life. But, fancy cars aside, I promise: more money does not equal more happiness.

On today's walk, think about your beliefs about money and happiness. Do you have enough money to cover your basic expenses? If not, can you adjust what you spend (fewer morning lattes) or what you make (side hustle anyone)?

More importantly, do you believe that more money will make you happier? Do you find yourself engaging in rounds of compare and despair, especially while scrolling social media?

Finally, consider the things that are most important to you, that you love about your life and for which you are grateful (yes, here we go on gratitude again). How many of those things are based on how much money you have? If you are like most people, not many.

● ● ●

Walk # 57: Pick Up the Dustball

Walking up the stairs in my house the other day, I noticed a ball of dust and dog hair in the corner of a step. I saw it out of the corner of my eye and kept walking. Later that afternoon, I noticed it again. And then again the next morning. And one more time before I finally picked it up.

Now in my defense, the first time I had walked up the stairs, I had something in my hands and the second time, I was on my way to do something. But, if I'm going to be really honest, with you and with myself, I just didn't feel like bending over and picking up the dustball.

Here's the thing: every time I noticed the dustball and didn't pick it up, I expended a tiny bit of my mental energy. I squandered a sliver of my focus. And every time I noticed it, but didn't bother to pick it up, I knew I was going to have to notice it again and think about it again until I did something about it.

Now sometimes, if you ignore the dustball, it will seem to go away, perhaps getting blown down the steps and under the couch where it will meet up with other dustballs and remain, happily just out of sight. But even though you can't see it, that dustball is still there and it can, in the most subtle and insidious ways, cause you trouble. It can trigger allergies or blow out from under the couch at the most inopportune moments, like when you have your mother-in-law over.

Now, just to be clear, we're not just talking about dustballs (though that thing with the dustball on the stairs really did happen). We are talking about the little, messy things that pop up in our lives that should be dealt with and addressed: the conversation you don't want to have, the project you don't want to do or the phone call you don't want to make. The nagging physical problem you don't want to call the doctor about. Ignored, dustballs get bigger and every time you notice them, they capture more of your valuable—and limited—mental energy.

We all have lots and lots of dustballs in our lives and when you let the dustballs pile up, your house gets messier and messier.

Dealing with your dustballs is critical to clearing the path to the life you want.

On today's walk, think about some dustballs you are dealing with in your own life right now. Difficult conversations you need to have that are lurking at the corner of your mind, which pop up from time to time in your mind, but that you keep pushing away. A physical issue that you've been ignoring, even though it continues to crop up from time to time. An area of your home that isn't as tidy or as organized as you wish that "bothers" you every time you notice it or think about it. Those are your dustballs. Make a commitment to picking them up and disposing of them properly.

● ● ●

Walk # 58: The Value of Doing Something Once

Nope, going to the gym once will not change your life. Or your body. Making time to call your mother once will not insulate you from future "you never call me" admonishments. Taking a single afternoon off to build a fort in the living room without worrying about the ensuing mess will not make you mom of the year.

So, does doing something just once have value? Is it worth going to the gym without making a "commitment" to go three times a week? Is it worth reining in your temper when you know you are likely to lose it some other time? Is it worth making time to get down on the floor and play with your kids today when you know that tomorrow you might be too busy? Is it worth heading out the door for a walk if you only have fifteen minutes when you had promised yourself you'd walk two miles each day?

Absolutely. We put so much pressure on ourselves to commit to big change and we've all "committed" and then fallen off one wagon or another. Many of us have fallen off the same wagon over and over. So we tell ourselves, consciously or not, that it's not worth making a commitment to change our diet, improve a troubled relationship, or parent with more patience because we fear not being able to "follow through."

But what if we decide that one positive act has value all on its own? What if we believe that putting even one instance of goodness out into the world is worthwhile? What if we stop putting so much pressure on ourselves to bring about a systemic change in our lives and simply do a positive and good thing for the sake of that one positive and good thing?

If we did, we could change our worlds. Because here's the thing: all change, all growth, all accomplishments are nothing more than the accumulation of hundreds of small steps and tiny actions in the right direction. Sustained relationships are built over time, one meaningful moment at a time. Businesses are built one customer at a time. Pounds are lost one meal at a time. Books are written one word at a time. Marathons are run one step at a time. Dogs are trained one treat at a time.

On today's walk, think about the times you have committed to "big" change and fallen off the wagon. Think about the person you want to be and the goals you want to crush and for today, just for today, make choices and take steps in that direction. Just for today. Worry about tomorrow, tomorrow.

Walk # 59: You Do You

When I was 23, I went sailing in the British Virgin Islands for three weeks with my then-husband. One afternoon, we dropped anchor at a small island that housed little more than a beach bar tended by a barefoot guy with long dreadlocks. We ordered their special cocktail—I recall something with nutmeg—and sat to watch the sunset. Moments later, a young boy scampered past, followed closely by a blond woman.

The story I was told is that the woman had visited this tiny island on holiday, met the owner of this little beach bar, fell in love, and never returned to her home in Canada. Instead, they married and were raising their family on that tiny island. It was the first time I saw someone who had simply said no to the traditional path that life had laid out for her.

At this very second, there are families living on boats sailing across the Caribbean and in RVs exploring the mid-west. There are women happily raising one kid, eight kids, or no kids. There are moms who are breastfeeding and moms who are bottle feeding. Women writing books and writing grant proposals to raise money for the not-for-profit they dreamed of. Right this very second, there are women hiking in the mountains of Tibet and camping in the mountains of Colorado.

Making the commitment to being the truest expression of yourself is hard. It requires you to look as honestly and objectively as possible at who you are, who you want to be, and what you want—really, truly want— out of your life. It requires facing your shortcomings and acknowledging your biggest dreams. There is a very good chance that it will require you to walk down a path that someone in your life doesn't approve of.

None of that is easy. First of all, we are all really, really busy. We run around getting things done, rarely stopping to consider whether all of those things we are doing are, in fact, worth doing.

Moreover, if you really stop to look at the life you want, you will be forced to confront the things in your life that are not in alignment with that vision. The relationships that aren't working, the work that isn't satisfying, the unwanted weight you are carrying, the dreams you cast aside. It is so, so easy to go through the motions. And it is so, so easy to conform to what society tells us we should be doing and how we should be living. As women, here are just a few of the things that society tells us:

- Study hard and get good grades
- Be polite
- Keep your home tidy
- Watch your weight
- Mascara and lipstick are essential
- Get an education, have a career
- Find your soulmate, get married, have a baby
- Keep working, because you can have it all
- Stop working because your family needs you
- Plastic is bad, and so are non-organic strawberries
- Have another baby

Society is tough. Society has a strong interest in maintaining the status quo, keeping things as they are, because those who are in charge like it that way.

Now for many, many of us—myself included—there are elements of what society has told us that really work for us. I did, in fact, go to school, get good grades, marry a great guy, and have two children. I started businesses that failed and a couple that succeeded. I live in a home I love, which I generally keep pretty tidy. Sometimes, I even wear mascara and lipstick.

But along the way, there were countless times when I was forced to look at what society was telling me to do and say no. I said no to a marriage that wasn't working (divorced at 26!), said no to a career that wasn't fulfilling (you can't walk away from a potential law firm partnership!), and adopted my second child (why would you want to adopt a child when you could "have one of your own?"). The list goes on. At the time, each of those choices was challenging. Each of those choices required that I look at the messages that I had been sent and say, "That is not my path." That is not easy. But it is the only way for you to do you.

On today's walk, let's look at things that you are doing—right now—because society, or your mother, or the media, is telling you that is what you are supposed to be doing. And then think about what you should be doing to be you.

● ● ●

Walk # 60: What I Learned from Josephine Fazio and Benjamin Franklin

I arrived at college barely seventeen and moved myself and my six large garbage bags of stuff into a shared room on Denton 8, the top floor of a dorm at the northwest edge of the University of Maryland. I recall feeling a little like I was at sea, like the world beneath my feet was unsteady. Slowly but surely, I got my bearings. I found my classes spread out across the 1,335-acre campus and found my first college friends just across the hall.

And then I got the flu. I recall laying in my single bed feeling sick and never so lonely in my life. When I was a very young child, I had an immune deficiency—my body didn't produce the natural immunity it should. Some doctors wanted to treat me with daily medication and others suggested I be kept away from other kids to avoid exposure to infection. One wise doctor told my mother to just "give her body a chance to figure it out." So that's what my parents did and throughout elementary school I caught one cold after another. I would lie in my parents' big bed and watch TV and they would bring me soup, orange juice, books, and games and nurture me until I was back on my feet. This happened a lot until my body's immune system kicked into gear. By the time I got to college, I had a lot of experience being sick.

But lying in my college dorm room, I realized that I had no experience being sick by myself. Alone. How does one get soup, juice, and water when your head feels like it weighs a thousand pounds? Was I really supposed to drag myself, alone, to the health center, which was a twenty minute walk away? Would anyone even notice if I just laid here and died?

And then Josephine knocked on my door. My across-the-hall neighbor, whom I barely knew. The middle daughter of a big Italian family, Jo knew a thing or two about taking care of people and about family and community. "Are you okay?" she asked. "What can I bring you from the dining hall?"

My stubborn, independent, left-high-school-just-after-her-seventeenth-birthday self, who was desperate to prove her independence almost said, "Nothing, I'm fine." But I didn't.

"Could you bring me some bread and something to drink?" I croaked.

Ten minutes later she was back with juice, water, bread, and a bowl of soup. And a spoon. And a napkin.

I learned a valuable lesson that day. First, Jo was a good friend. Second, if you ask for help, there are likely to be people who will help.

We are all running around acting like "we've got this." We don't need anyone. We don't need any help. We think that we are supposed to be able to do it all and that asking for help means we are weak or have failed.

But here's the secret. None of us can do it all. None of us have it all together. Every one of sometimes feels overwhelmed. Every one of us has bad days. Every one of us needs help.

Here's another fact: People want to help you and are happy to help you. In fact—and this may sound remarkable—but research shows that people who have done you a favor are more likely to like you. This is because of a psychological phenomenon called "The Franklin Effect," named for Benjamin Franklin who wrote about an experience he had trying to win over a political rival. His tactic? He asked to borrow a rare book from the man, who agreed. Franklin returned the book with a heartfelt note of appreciation. That simple exchange changed their relationship—the man became friendly and ultimately an ally of Franklin. This phenomenon has been tested by researchers who reached the same conclusion—doing a favor for someone makes you feel more kindly toward them.

Now I'm not suggesting that you ask for favors with the goal of turning your adversaries into your allies, although apparently, that is possible. Rather, if you are reluctant to ask for help because you fear it will cause people to think poorly of you or dislike you, rest assured, the exact opposite is likely to be true.

On today's walk, think about the times that you've needed help but declined to ask for it and then make a commitment to ask for help when you need it—and offer help when you can.

Walk # 61: 100 Years, All New People

With a small handful of exceptions, in 100 years, this planet will be inhabited by all new people. Not by us, nor by our children. Things are ever-changing all around us, despite how much we wish to hold on to the things we love. As much as we hold our children close and long to keep them small and under our roof, they are growing before our eyes. As much as we want to hold on to our parents, their time with us is limited. And ourselves? Yup, us too.

Now I get that thinking about the impermanence of it all can launch many of us into an existential crisis and a fear of change that keeps us up at night. But surrendering to the reality of those inevitable changes can have three profound and positive influences in our lives.

The truth is that most of what we worry about, fret about, and get upset about is, in the grand scheme of things, entirely irrelevant. When little Timmy won't put his socks on and that makes us late to little Betsy's ballet class, well... 100 years, all new people. The roof that has been leaking off and on for 18 months? 100 years, all new people. The guy who cuts you off on your way to work or the woman who steals your parking spot at the grocery store? 100 years, all new people.

When we allow fret and worry to consume precious moments of our life, we sacrifice joy. When we allow petty annoyances to get under our skin, we let other people rob us of happiness. And either way, 100 years, all new people.

Accepting the reality of our limited time here can—and should—compel us to live more mindfully. I recall one day I was standing in the shower with clean, hot water bathing my body. It was late afternoon and the sun was streaming through the window, turning the shower spray into a thousand tiny rainbows and I felt profoundly lucky to be there, in that moment, with the great fortune to live in a time and a place where I can simply turn a knob and bathe myself in clean, hot water. When we race from one thing to another, we are missing out on the moments that make all of those tasks worthwhile. Remembering that our time here is limited can infuse your days with a greater sense of awareness and appreciation.

Finally, accepting the stark limitations of our time here reminds us that we have a limited opportunity to leave an imprint by making this world a better place. There's an interesting exercise that encourages people to take a few minutes to write their own eulogy and, while I find the practice a little creepy, the concept is a sound one. Few of us ever take a moment to think about the legacy or impact we would like to leave. So, if you can without it sending you spinning, consider what you hope people would say about you when you are gone.

I am pretty confident that not a single one of us would hope that as our loved ones reflect on our time together, they would say "She was so busy." Rather, most of us would hope that they would say something more along the lines of "She lived with a full heart" or "She touched those around her" or "She made the world a better place." Once you have clarity around the legacy you hope to leave, it is easier to live your life in a way that aligns with that vision.

Many of us rush through life in part because we are afraid to come face to face with the impermanence of it all. I get it, I truly do. But if we take a deep breath and accept that in 100 years it will be all new people populating this planet, living in our towns, perhaps even living in our homes, it can have a profound and positive impact on how we live our lives.

On today's walk, think about some of the things that annoy you during the course of a typical day and try to reframe them in the context of 100 years, all new people. Strive to tap into a heightened level of mindfulness by taking in the sun or the clouds, the feel of the air on your skin, the sound of your footsteps. Finally, think a bit about your legacy, what you truly wish to leave behind.

Walk # 62: Clear the Clutter

When people walk into our house, they often remark on the lack of "stuff" we have laying around. "But where's your pile of mail?" Mary asked last time she visited. "And where are the kids' toys?"

It's not that I'm a clean freak who runs around picking up after my family or spends hours each day straightening up my house because truly, I do neither. But I have made a conscious and deliberate decision to reduce the amount of clutter in my life.

The Merriam Webster Dictionary defines clutter:

"scattered or disordered things that impede movement or reduce effectiveness" or *"interfering radar echoes caused by reflection from objects (as on the ground) other than the target."*

I love *so much* about this definition of clutter. Let's think about this a little bit. Clutter impedes your movement, reduces your effectiveness and interferes with your ability to stay locked on your target. Most of us have filled our lives with clutter that needs to be cleared away to give us the space to live the life we really want.

Clutter comes in essentially three places: our stuff, our calendar, and our to-do list. The only way you will move freely toward your goals without interference is to reduce the clutter in all three of those aspects of your life.

Your Stuff

We all have too much stuff. Even I, someone who is constantly looking to keep the clutter from getting the best of me, just counted a total of 37 towels in a house of four people. (Yes, I just ran around to each closet and bathroom and counted). That is about nine towels per person, and that is ridiculous.

You should surround yourself with only two categories of things. First, things you truly need and use on a regular basis. Second, stuff that makes you happy or, in the words of Marie Kondo, author of *The Life-Changing Magic of Tidying Up,* that give you joy. Everything else... anything that you don't use regularly or that doesn't give you joy is simply standing in the way.

Your Calendar

Oh, the commitments we make. Oh, how good it feels to be asked, "Could you help with the PTA bake sale? You're so good at things like that."

Yes, it is good to be wanted. Yes, it is hard to say no.

I just counted and I have fifteen things on my calendar for the day. Fifteen calls and appointments. There is, objectively, no way that I can be effective in fifteen calls or meetings. No way. And yet there they are, screaming back at me from a calendar that I created. That I filled. Fifteen things. Some of them are directly related to my goals and some of them are simply things I have to do (gyno anyone?). But so many of the others are there because I didn't want to say no when someone asked me.

Your calendar should have two things: things that either move you one step closer to your goals or things that bring you joy and happiness. Okay, well, not the gyno—some things you just have to do if you are going to be a grown-up who takes care of herself and her family. But the other stuff? Don't let other people decide how you are going to spend your time. Don't let your calendar become filled with clutter that impedes your movement forward or interferes with your focus on your target.

Your To-Do List

My lists have lists. And that is due in part of the fact that I have found that capturing ideas onto a list helps to get them out of my head. As a self-aware "idea junkie" I know that when I have an idea, it will rattle around in my mind until I get it down on paper (or on my digital to-do list). But here's the problem: so many of those ideas are clutter.

Here's how I manage that.

First, you need to create a to-do list someplace that is really convenient for you. I use an app that syncs to all of my devices. Then, you need to get every idea down on that list. That will free your mind. But then (and here's the part that is most challenging for me) you need to break that list into: (1) mission-critical, (2) must get done, and (3) maybe someday. I have another list called "waiting for" where I put things that I'm waiting for from other people.

Mission-critical items are the things that are most important for your goal. It could be work related or it could be planning a fabulous sixth birthday party for little Timmy. These are your most important things right now.

"Must get done" are the things that, well, must get done as a grown-up. Like scheduling that appointment with the gyno.

"Maybe someday" are the things that you'd like to do, maybe, but that don't currently align with your most important things. Ideas you don't want to forget. Things you'd like to do and like to accomplish.

Start with the mission-critical. Then, once a week, at a regularly scheduled time (I do it Friday at 3:00), review all of your lists, including the maybe someday, because sometimes those ideas have become mission-critical.

On today's walk, think about where you have the clutter in your life, is it your stuff, your calendar or your to-do list? When you get back, begin dealing with that specific clutter, one small step at a time.

Walk # 63: The Critical Importance of Confidence

When I was in fourth grade, all of the girls auditioned for chorus. One by one, we stood in front of the class while Mrs. Stang, the music teacher, sat at the piano. She played a few notes and we each sang a few bars of "My Country 'Tis Of Thee." Three days later, she posted the list of the girls who made chorus. That list included all but three of the fourth grade girls. I was one of the three left off the list. The three of us who weren't invited to join chorus had recess outside, which you'd think would have been a good thing. But it wasn't. We sat outside, feeling desperately left out.

My parents were outraged. They called the school—something they rarely did, because they were generally of the mind that kids do need to face some challenges and navigate some waters on their own.

The next day after music class, Mrs. Stang asked me to stay after class. This is it, I thought. She's going to tell me she made a mistake and invite me to join the chorus. Here's what she said instead, "You can't carry a tune and you can't be in chorus. But if you want to stay after school and work with me, I'll see if I can help you."

I was devastated and I haven't sung since. Well, okay, I sing if I'm alone in my car but that's pretty much it. Yup, I'm the person who only pretends to sing Happy Birthday, silently mouthing the words. Even at my own kids' birthday parties.

So, here's the thing that sucks. At some point in your life, someone told you weren't good at something. Or, you failed at something that was important to you.

But your ability to achieve your goals, to have the life you want begins with your belief in your ability to do it. No matter what it is. Whether it is singing happy birthday, getting the job of your dreams, building a business, writing a book, or roasting a turkey, confidence is critical.

There are so many things that can affect your confidence. Parents who didn't tell you how awesome you were as a child, "friends" who feel better by making you feel worse, husbands who take you down instead of build you up, magazines that make it all look easy and perfect… the images are all around us and, compared to them, we will never measure up. Because they are NOT REAL.

Confidence is eroded by the perceived failure to live up to some mysterious, unattainable image of the perfect. Confidence can only come from inside. It can be built in small increments by small successes. It can be nurtured by forgiving yourself your mistakes, setting reasonable expectations, and inviting people into your life who build you up and don't take you down into their lives.

And (this is really important) confidence often requires a conscious act of will. Now I know that you look around you and see people who you are sure never suffer from moments of self-doubt. People who ooze success and confidence. But here's the truth—everyone has insecurities. Everyone has moments of doubt. You do, and they do. The key is being willing to stand up, take the chance, learn the lessons, and move forward in spite of those feelings of doubt. Because once the success starts coming, the confidence will begin to build. And then you will be unstoppable.

On today's walk, think about moments in your life when you accomplished something you set out to do, achieved a goal, or experienced success. Let your mind wander onto all of your accomplishments. If your mind tries to turn to things that haven't gone as planned, bring it back. When you get back, capture a list of those successes below. Next time you think "I can't," read the list of "I did."

● ● ●

Walk # 64: You Want to be President? You Mean of the PTA, Right?

Here's the truth: most of us go through life sucked deep into the whirlwind, rarely allowing ourselves to think about our big dreams or huge goals. They are usually still there, lurking at the edges of our minds, a distant memory of the dreams and aspirations we had when we were younger when the world seemed to brim with possibilities. But then three things come along to kill our dreams.

Of Course You Can Be President, Honey!

A fascinating thing happens as people grow up. When children express their dreams, adults typically cheer them on. "Of course you can be president," we say with a smile. "You can be anything you want," we promise. And a part of us believes that. After all, someone has to grow up to be president. Why not our precious little Susie?

But when that same child is heading off to college and trying to decide on a field of study and says, "I'm going to study political science," how many adults will ask, "What are you going to DO with a degree in political science?" And when that optimistic eighteen-year old says, "I'm going to be president," well... imagine the eye rolls.

Now let's imagine that Susie graduated from college, worked for a few years in Washington and then took eight years off to raise her kids. Imagine if, over coffee last week, she said, "I want to be president." Assume she was thirty-two-years-old and the mother to two small children. You would think she was crazy. You would think, even if you didn't say it, *"There's no way."* You might even laugh a little until you looked into her eyes and realized she was serious.

Now here's the thing: someone has done these things to *you* in *your* life. Someone has told you that your dreams are too big. Too impossible. Someone has told you that you are not good enough, smart enough, or special enough.

Failure Sucks

In Walk #26, we talked about how much failure sucks. We start out on a new path or new project with hope and optimism. With a desire to make change or accomplish something awesome. And then we fail. If we are lucky, we fail over and over because that means we are continuing to try new things and take new chances.

But usually each failure is accompanied by a scar. And those scars add up in the form of a little voice that, when you try again, begins to say *"you've failed before, so what makes you think this time will be any different?"* That little voice makes you hold back a little more each time, investing a little bit less ambition into whatever project or dream you are hoping for. The book you are holding in your hands right this very second is proof that that voice must be ignored. This is the eleventh book I've started. Three works of fiction were completed, but none were published. Seven non-fiction books were started and never completed. That is a whole lot of failure. That is a big, loud voice in my head that I have chosen to consciously ignore.

Oh, The Whirlwind

The pressure of the adult whirlwind, especially when you are also raising a family, is very, very real. We are constantly working to pay the bills and get dinner on the table. If you have toddlers, the day to day challenge of simply keeping them alive during the toddler stage, which I call "full mobility, no judgment," can be all-consuming. I remember a day when my daughter was about two and we were standing at the top of the stairs in our old house. She lifted her arms high into the air and launched herself forward. The only thing that I can think is that she was trying to discover whether or not she could fly. Full mobility, no judgment. Fortunately, I was right there to catch her. But truthfully, that morning could have ended very differently. If you find yourself in that stage right now, well, I hear you. I feel you.

The whirlwind is real, but it is no reason to give up on your dreams. How? First, recognize that this stage will pass, probably more quickly than you can possibly imagine while you are in it. And there are many, many things you can do to keep the whirlwind at bay while you drive your dreams forward. For starters, focus on your 3Fs and always be developing skills and competencies that will help you not just for the life you are living now but also for the life you want to be living in three to five years. Second, be precious about your time and your time commitments. Say no to things that don't either move your closer to your dreams or feed your spirit.

There is no easy answer to this. Chasing your dreams as an adult requires a serious act of will.

On today's walk, think about your big dreams. Maybe it is that book. Maybe it is a Hawaiian vacation. Maybe it is becoming a CPA, artist, or teacher. Maybe it is opening a school for differently-abled children or speaking on stage in front of 1,000 people. Tune back into your dream.

Walk # 65: How to Silence the Naysayers

On our last walk, we considered our big dreams and the whirlwind that can stand in our way. For many of us, roadblocks are also created by the naysayers in our lives.

When I was a young lawyer, one of the hottest shows on television was "LA Law." It was a character-driven drama set in a small Los Angeles law firm. I had watched every episode since the premiere and knew the characters well. One of my best high school friends had moved to LA after college to pursue a career as a talent agent and managed to score a job at a top agency.

She called me one day and said, "You should write a spec script for 'LA Law.' You know the show so well, and you're a great writer. I know someone there, and I can get it read. Who knows?" she said. "Maybe they'll buy it, and if they love it, maybe they'll hire you."

And, because I am usually up for a challenge, I've always loved to write, and the thought of getting hired as a writer for "LA Law" was downright intoxicating, I said "I'm on it. Can you send me some samples so I can see the format?"

I went home that night incredibly excited. While I loved my job (I know that's weird, most young lawyers do not love their jobs, but I did), the thought of creating a storyline and writing the dialogue for my favorite characters was intoxicating. And here's where this story goes bad. I repeated my entire conversation with Heidi to my (then) husband and told him my plan. He looked at me and said, "What makes you think you can do that? You don't know anything about writing a script."

I went ahead and wrote it anyway, and six weeks later, I sent it off to Heidi who managed to get it read by the team at LA Law. They didn't produce my story, and they didn't hire me. But I wrote an entire spec script for my favorite television show.

Yet my ex-husband's words rang in my head: "What makes you think you can do that?"

I do not doubt that there are people in your life who have said: "What makes you think you can do that?" Perhaps not in those words.

Maybe they've said it in the way they cock their head slightly when you share your dream and they look at you just a little funny. Perhaps they ask seemingly well-meaning questions like "How are you going to do that? You are already so busy with your kids." Or maybe they say something like "Wow, good for you. I could never do anything like that; my kids are my priority right now."

We could spend some time playing psychologist and try to figure out why people feel they need to crush your dreams, keep you on the ground, or hold you back. Maybe it's their fear of losing you. Maybe your big dreams make them feel less than you. Maybe they are trying to protect you from the pain of the failure that is inevitable along the path to big dreams. Maybe they simply can't understand your dreams and ambition.

Truly, it doesn't matter. What matters is that no one has the right to tell you that you are not entitled to your dreams. No one has the right to question your passion or ability to chase and conquer your dream, whatever it may be. Everyone has a dream. Everyone's dream looks different. Your dream is unique to you. And that means that you are uniquely qualified to chase it.

My ex-husband was right. At the moment that Heidi suggested I write a spec script for "LA Law," I didn't know how to do it. But I learned. And if writing for television in Los Angeles had been my dream, I would have continued to learn and grow and pursue that dream until I mastered that craft and crushed that dream.

How do we manage the naysayers? Truthfully, it isn't easy. Usually, it requires an act of will. It requires you to look at the naysayers, the negative nellies, the critical people, the unsupportive people, the people who will suck the wind from your sails and consciously think: "You do not understand how strong I am. You do not understand my dream. And that's okay, because this is my dream, not yours." And then you have to go forward and work, maybe every day, to silence the naysayers.

On today's walk, think about the naysayers in your life. Yes, they might be people you love. And they might be people who love you. But in order to manage them, first you have to recognize them.

● ● ●

Walk # 66: Be Brave

Changing your life requires one huge act of bravery followed by a thousand small acts of bravery.

The initial huge act of bravery is often done quietly, happening privately and without much fanfare. In fact, no one will even know that you are being brave. It is an invisible act of bravery. You must be brave enough to decide that there is something in your life that you want to change, perhaps your job, weight, happiness, relationship, where you live, the work you do, or the people you hang out with. If there is something in your life that you want—or need—to change, the very first thing you must do is decide. Decide that you've had enough. Decide that you want something different. Making that decision is the first crucial act of bravery.

Just because it is silent bravery doesn't mean it isn't scary. If you have tried a hundred times to change your body and get healthy, making the decision to change your body and get healthy—again—is terrifying. Making the decision to change your career or land a new job or make a material shift in your relationship is terrifying. Deciding to adopt a child or give up your teaching job or become a writer? Terrifying.

Why does making the decision to change your life require an act of bravery?

Because change is scary. Change brings unpredictability and, as humans, we are wired to like predictability because predictable is safe. Because change thrusts you into the unknown, and the unknown is scary.

We tend to think of acts of bravery as big things often done in public. Jumping out of an airplane, walking on stage and speaking in front of 500 people, leading an army into battle. But making decisions that put the wheels in motion to create change in your life, to step outside your comfort zone, to strive for bigger, better, or different, that is being brave in your heart.

We do ourselves a disservice when we don't recognize and honor those initial acts of bravery. That first step. So, how do you become brave enough to take that first step?

There are two ways.

First, you can become so sick and tired of the way things are that you simply feel like you have no choice. You can choose to wait until you are burned out, hit rock bottom, or become desperate. That's okay, sometimes bravery comes from a place of desperation. Other times, a brave decision comes from a place of deliberately deciding that it is time for a change and that you are willing to take the risk.

We've talked a lot about failure, both the importance of and the risks. As much as you can remind yourself that risk is the entrance fee to success, it is nevertheless, scary stuff.

Taking risks and, therefore, making changes, requires bravery. Quiet, powerful bravery. How?

You need to scare yourself by looking really, really hard at what happens if you don't make that change. Yes, change thrusts you into the world of the unknown. You don't know where you will be in one year or five years or twenty years. But will your life be the life you truly want? Will you end up with regrets and what-ifs? If so, you need to be scared of *that*. You need to be as afraid to walk away from this life with regrets as you are brave enough to take the chances that will help get you where you want to go.

No one wants to look at that. No one wants to close their eyes and picture themselves in the nursing home rocking chair, a knit blanket on their lap, contemplating their life. No one wants to go to that place in their mind. Why? Because it is terrifying.

So be brave and go there with me.

On today's walk, picture yourself in that rocking chair with that knit blanket on your lap. Let's put that rocker on a lovely front porch so it's not quite as scary. Looking back on your life, what do you see? Are they what you want to see? What are the accomplishments that were important to you? What was most meaningful to you? Where are the cherished moments?

Walk # 67: How to Bounce

It would be fantastic if we could just shake off our failures and disappointments instantly without skipping a beat. Unfortunately, navigating failure is more nuanced than that. Failure feels bad. It dampens your spirit and causes you to question your path, your choices, or, worst of all, your abilities. If you are going to chase big dreams, you need a toolbox of tactics to manage the stumbles and setbacks you will encounter along the way. Without it, those setbacks can destroy your dreams.

Over the past decade, I've asked dozens of successful, high-performing women how they manage "those days" and bounce back from setbacks. Though everyone works through their failures a bit differently, there are several consistent tactics to how they manage to keep standing back up.

First, give yourself permission to catch your breath and lick your wounds, but put a time limit on it. Mindy Scheier is the founder of Runway of Dreams, a non-profit that offered the world's first mainstream adaptive clothing line, inspired by her disabled son. She says, "We all have those days when we want to put our heads down on the table. I allow myself those days, but give myself a finite amount of time—usually one day—and then I just get back up." You do need time to process what happened and recover your energy. Give yourself that time, but no longer.

Second, practice a little self-care. You took a fall and are a bit bumped and bruised. Though you might feel you don't "deserve" a long soak in a bubble bath, an afternoon walk in the woods, or a sumptuous dinner, you do. You tried something. You took a swing. It didn't work out. You deserve to nurture those wounds in whatever way helps you feel better.

Third, be very mindful of your self-talk. When things don't go as planned, many of us become our own biggest critics. "*I should have seen it coming.*" "*I wasn't prepared.*" Or worse is some version of my personal favorite: "*I suck.*" Yup, it is possible that you made a mistake, but if your kid made a mistake you wouldn't look at her and say "you suck," so don't say that to yourself. You are allowed to make mistakes. Truly, you are.

Fourth, remember that we all have them. No one has achieved anything awesome without a trail of failures behind them. Michael Jordan was cut from his high school basketball team. Lady Gaga was dropped by her first record label. Thomas Edison was told that he was stupid. Steven King's first book was rejected 30 times. Your failure is just one in a long history of failures that have been the precursor to success.

Fifth, write it down. Writing is one of the very best ways for your brain to organize and process an experience. Don't edit, don't worry about spelling or punctuation, and don't write for anyone else. Let whatever is going to come, come. If you want to write about how awful the experience was, go for it. If you want to write about how you feel, that's good too. Let your mind follow whatever path it wants to lead you down, but get it on paper.

Sixth, don't catastrophize. It is so easy, especially at 2:00 a.m., to allow your mind to envision a snowball effect of a single setback. Don't do it.

Seventh, as soon as possible, take action. As soon as you have given yourself your allotted recovery time—be it an evening, a day, or a weekend—force yourself to get up and start doing things. Take action toward your goal. One step. Then two steps. Make the next call, send the next email, ask the next question, or book the next conference.

Finally, focus on others. Someone needs you. Your team, your kids, your spouse, your PTA, or your neighbor who is battling breast cancer. Show up for them.

On today's walk, think about your playbook for failure because even if you are not wrestling with a failure or setback right now, if you are swinging big, taking chances, and chasing your dreams, there are setbacks coming. And there is no better time to plan for how you are going to manage setbacks than when you are *not* in the throes of one.

●●●

Walk # 68: Time for Some Tough Love

To paraphrase speaker and author Mel Robbins, getting what you want is simple, but it's not easy.

Let me tell you how simple it is. If you want to lose weight you need to eat less and move more. If you want to write a book, you need to sit down every day and write between 500 and 1,000 words. If you want a better job, you need to develop the skills you will need for that job and then interview, network and interview some more. If you want a new relationship, you need to go out and meet new people. If you want to be a better mom, you need to take better care of yourself so that you have more to give.

For pretty much everything you want, there is a clear path to achieving it. Even big things. If you want to bring fresh water to communities in Africa, there is a path to that. If you want to bring clothing and shoes to the poorest people in the Dominican Republic, you can do that too.

But oh, how we can make excuses. And your excuses are untrue.

Excuse #1: If Only My Husband Would Drive More Carpools…

Even if we don't say it aloud, and even if we barely acknowledge it ourselves, we often blame other people for our inability to get what we want. *"If only my husband would take more responsibility for the kids, I would have more time to study for my CPA exam." "If only I didn't have to feed my kids, I'd be able to keep the junk out of the house and lose weight." "If only I had more friends willing to help me, I'd be able to start that foundation I've always dreamed of starting."* And you are probably right. If your husband made more lunches or drove more carpools, you might have more time. If you kept the junk food out of the house, you might have an easier time losing weight. And a supportive, engaged friend group could help you launch that non-profit. But if you wait for other people to help you start on the path to achieving your goals, then you are going to wait a long, long time. These are your goals, dreams, and ambitions and you need to take ownership of them. You—and you alone—will need to do the work to achieve them. Now that's not to say that you don't need help and support along the way—you do and you will. But it means that you can't expect anyone else to do the work necessary to get you there. It's on you, sister.

Excuse #2: If Only I Had More Time...

We are all busy. In fact, we are all too busy. But we are busy as a consequence of our own doing. We say yes when we should say no. We fill our days with other people's obligations and agendas. And believe me, I understand this better than anyone. I am the poster child for the overcommitted, busy person who often fills her days with too much. You have to make time to devote to your priorities and your goals. In Walk #3, we talked about ways you could recover fifteen-minute increments to devote toward your goal. Go back and look at the list you created, add anything you missed, and get serious about devoting that time to your goals.

Excuse #3: If Only I Had More Money...

You'd be surprised how often I hear this. But money does not buy dreams. In fact, it is the other way around. Wanting more money, wanting a bigger life, wanting more opportunities for you and your family—those are reasons to double-down on chasing your dreams.

Your excuses are just that: excuses. Yup, it's possible that if certain things were different in your life, it would be easier to chase your dreams. But having a big life and accomplishing what you want to accomplish is not going to be easy. Simple, yes. Possible, yes. But not easy. No one is going to do it for you. And it is never too late to start, but we'll talk about that on our next walk.

On today's walk, ask yourself what excuses you are making. Who are you blaming? What are you letting stand in your way? We all have them. We all make them. What are yours?

● ● ●

Walk # 69: It's Never Too Late To Start

I was a first-year law student sitting in Civil Procedure trying to unravel the mysteries of federal jurisdiction when it occurred to me that it was too late for me to become an Olympic... well, an Olympic anything. And being in the Olympics seemed like a really cool experience. And I was still so young. But I realized that it was too late for me to be an Olympian. Now, despite the fact that I'd always been active and athletic, I had never participated in any competitive sport. Never. Yet there I was, freaking out because it occurred to me that it was too late for me to become an Olympian. That door was closed to me, and I have struggled to keep the feeling of closing doors at bay ever since.

I suspect, like me, you have sometimes felt that it is too late to start a new project or to chase a new dream. It's not surprising. We live in a society that glorifies college students who made millions from their dorm rooms and bombards us with images of airbrushed 18-year-olds.

There's more. As years go by, we have experiences that teach us that things don't always go as planned, dreams don't always come true, and when you take chances, sometimes you fail. Finally, there is the reality of our adult lives and the whirlwind in which most of us live. It seems just about impossible to add one more thing to our plates or when most of us are simply struggling to keep our heads above water.

If you are over 30—much less over 40—it is easy to believe that your best years are behind you and that the door to your dreams has slammed shut.

They haven't. How do I know? Well, here are eight incredibly accomplished people who didn't start racking up the wins until after 40.

Grandma Moses, one of the nation's most iconic folk artists, didn't begin painting until she was 78. 78!

Mary Kay Ash launched her business with a vision and $5,000 when she was 45 years old.

Julia Child published her first cookbook at 50.

Laura Ingalls Wilder published Little House in the Big Woods at 65.

Ray Kroc founded McDonald's at 59.

Samuel L. Jackson didn't get his first big acting break until he was 43.

And do you remember Susan Boyle, the odd woman with the frizzy hair who showed up on *Britain's Got Talent* and sang her heart out? She was 47 and went on to release best-selling album after album and perform for the Queen.

And then there is my parents' friend Carolyn who launched her first business, a franchise that brings early STEM education to preschoolers, at age 89. In fabulous shoes. After kicking cancer's ass in her 70s.

As long as you have breath in your lungs, you have time to chase your dreams and to do the work to create the life you want.

I recently researched the oldest people to compete in the Olympics and discovered that there are many Olympians in their 50s, several in their 60s, and even a few who competed in their 70s. Maybe my Olympic dreams aren't dead yet.

On today's walk, think about the dreams you tell yourself it is too late for you to chase, pursue, or have. Get real here, and when you get back, write them down and take a good hard look. If it's not too late to go the Olympics, it's not too late to write the book, move to the beach, visit Asia, or become a CPA.

Walk # 70: A Blueprint for Goal Crushing

Did you know that oodles of research has revealed exactly what it takes for people to achieve their goals? There is a blueprint and, remarkably, it's all pretty straightforward.

Here's the secret sauce. The blueprint. The elements of goal crushing that hundreds of experts have proven to work.

Step One: Define a Measurable and Time-Bound Goal

If you don't know where you are going, then you will get lost along the way. Many of us are afraid to actually define a goal because if you don't actually set a goal, you can't fail. Get over that. Take a risk. Take a leap. Decide what you want.

When you define your goal, be sure it is measurable and time-bound.

Measurable means you will know exactly when you've achieved it. For example, "I want to get my bachelor's degree" is measurable. "I want to improve my education" is not. "I want to save $1,000 is measurable." "I want to save money" is not.

Your goal must also be time-bound which is a fancy way of saying it must have a deadline. "I want to save $1,000 by the end of the year" is time-bound.

Step Two: Find Your Why and Include People You Love

While the formula is simple, achieving big goals is hard and research shows that you have a better chance of getting there if the goal is something you want for you *and* for someone you love. Yup, we are hard-wired to be pretty decent beings who work harder for other people than we do for ourselves. For instance, if your goal is to lose 50 pounds this year for the sake of improving your own health, you are more likely to accomplish that goal if you add your kids to your why: "I will lose 50 pounds this year so that I can really get out and play with my kids at the playground" or "so that I will be able to dance at my daughter's wedding."

Step Three: Write It Down

Manifest that goal. Write it down, and, while you are at it, add your why. Yes, you can keep your goals digitally and there are so, so many apps and programs that purport to help you plan and achieve your goals. But what can I say... I don't think anything beats an old-fashioned notebook and pen. On Walk #41, we talked about your Goalpost Notebook. Write your goal in big letters on the first page.

On the next page, write your why. Be expansive and personal. Remember, this Goalpost Notebook is just for you. Get real with yourself. Really real.

Step Four: Phone a Friend

Now, while your Goalpost Notebook is personal, sharing your goal makes it more likely that you will achieve it. This is hard to do. Many of us keep our goals locked deep inside us. We don't tell a soul because if you say it aloud, you run the risk of public failure. Telling people makes you accountable. But here's the thing: if you are serious about achieving this goal, then you should share it with pride, excitement, and enthusiasm. Remember, the people who love you will want to see you succeed. Let them help inspire and support you. That said, if there are dream crushers in your life who tend to hold you back, let's just leave them out of this.

Step Five: Break It Down

Here's where things start to get interesting. Every goal is the result of a hundred or a thousand small steps. Small goals. Small actions. You need to identify those actions and begin crushing them, one small step at a time. You need to embrace the journey, day by day, while keeping your gaze on the goal in the distance. How?

Begin by starting your action list in your Goalpost Notebook. This will be a long, growing, living list of all of the steps you need to take to move toward your goal. I say living because often one step will lead to another that perhaps you didn't see at first.

Begin by listing all of the things you can possibly think of that are steps toward your goal. Remember, they need to be actionable, meaning things you can *do*. So, an action item is not "lose two pounds" on your way to losing 50, but it could be "walk a mile after dinner five evenings a week."

Step Six: Do the Work

Goals don't take care of themselves. Every single day you need to check in with your Goalpost Notebook and take steps toward your goal. Every. Single. Day. I get it, life can get in the way. Work blows up, kids get sick, and snow days happen.

You can manage all of those things and still move forward. I promise. All you need to do is prioritize your goal—cut down on the television and social media, get up 30 minutes earlier, or say no to something you don't really want to do. And remember, some steps toward your goal are likely to be small, simple, and quick. There is always some step forward that you can take. Always.

On today's walk, choose one goal that is really important to you. Just one. When you get back, capture your thoughts on taking these six steps below, or better yet... in your Goalpost Notebook.

Walk # 71: Objects in the Rearview Mirror... Should be Left There

Twelve years ago, I made a choice. I had been offered a job as the trustee for a large trust. It would have offered tremendous autonomy and responsibility. It wasn't work that was particularly interesting to me and it would have involved a lot of travel—not the fun kind. The salary was... wait for it... $300,000. And I turned it down. Can you imagine? Seriously, I can't either. But I turned it down because at the exact moment that opportunity came to me, we had just launched Macaroni Kid and *that* was my dream—to empower women across the country, to support and enrich local communities, to create opportunities, and to build a company unlike any other. So, I turned the job offer down.

Building a business has been much harder than I ever imagined. I've been through more sleepless nights than I can count and shed more tears than I can measure. I've worried about making payroll, paying my mortgage, and have given up worrying about retirement because that's not happening.

So, there are days when I wish I had taken that job. There are days when I head out for a walk and allow myself to get lost in the fantasy of what my life could have looked like had I taken that job.

But then I think about the adventures I've had, the people I've met and the families our company has impacted. I think about the notes of thanks I've received and the lifelong friendships that have been created in the Macaroni Kid community.

But sometimes, I still look backward. Sometimes, I still think *what if?*

It's no wonder that, when we are feeling low or stressed or sad, we indulge in a fantasy about how much better our life would be, how much happier we'd be, how much more successful we'd be had we only made that one different choice.

But.

Looking backward is absolutely no help. None. "I should have," "I could have," or "I wish I had," will get you nowhere. It will not help you move forward. It is like a dog licking a wound until it becomes red and inflamed. Yup, it might feel good for a second because it lets you indulge in a few minutes of what your life could have looked like. But it does not help.

And that fantasy vision you have of what your life would look like had you made that different choice? It's just a fantasy. You have *no idea* what your life would look like now had you made a different choice then, and any efforts to try are going to be riddled with revisionist history and fantasy. So whatever fantasy life you envision when you allow yourself to indulge in the *what-if* game has absolutely no basis in reality.

More importantly, every second you spend looking backward is a second you are not spending being grateful for the life you have, planning for the future you want, and actively working toward those dreams. You don't have time to look backward.

How do you avoid the temptation to indulge in the "what if" fantasies? First, when you find yourself thinking that way, immediately remind yourself that the perfect life you are envisioning is a fantasy. Second, take an action toward your goal or dream: send the email, make the call, take a walk, register for a webinar, write a paragraph of your book, or bake a cake. And, finally, by sheer act of will, you have to stop. Truly, though it might take some practice, you can control where you let your mind go, what you choose to fixate on, and what you are thinking about.

The business of living with intention, chasing dreams, and not giving up is hard. It doesn't afford you time to waste looking backward or second-guessing the decisions you've made. If something is working right now, don't look back, look forward.

And yup, some days, I need to take my own advice.

On today's walk, think about how often you look in the rearview mirror and think "what if?" And then make a conscious decision to, instead, set your sights on where you are going and focus on the future.

Walk # 72: Here's Why You're Afraid to Fail

The value of failure is all the rage. Fail forward, they tell us. Fail early and fail often. Failure is the greatest teacher. Everywhere we look we are being encouraged to swing big and fail hard.

If we accept that failure is the single best way to learn new lessons, explore new things and move us closer to the life we want, then why are we so afraid of it? Why don't we take bigger risks and bigger swings? Why don't we go after the things and the lives we want? Why do we settle? What exactly is it that we are so afraid of? Three things.

Reason One: I Might Learn Something About Myself That I Don't Want to Know

We are afraid that if we fail, it will prove to ourselves that we are failures. "See, I knew I couldn't lose the weight." "See, I knew I wasn't smart enough." "See, I knew I wasn't good enough for that new job, new career or better life."

Stop it. Taking a chance, setting a goal, trying something new, chasing a dream, those are not things you do once. Those are things you do-over and over and over. Trying and failing does not make you a failure. It means you tried something that didn't work. So try something else. Until it does. Do not let one failure, two failures, or ten failures convince you that you are a failure.

Reason Two: What Will They Think?

Okay, so here's the truth: there is a very good chance that you are not as afraid of failing as you are afraid of what other people are going to think about your failure. You are afraid of their judgment. You are afraid that they will talk about you, cluck their tongues, or look down their noses. You are afraid that they will think less of you.

Friends. Family members. Your mother-in-law. Your sister. Your neighbor. Your high school rival. Your children. It is *embarrassing* to fail.

But here's the thing. Would you ever tell your kid "No, Johnny, I don't think you should try out for the baseball team because what will the neighbors think if you don't make it"? That's insane. We'd never tell our kids that. We tell our children to go for it. We say, "Who cares what they think?"

And then what do we do if Johnny tries out for the baseball team and doesn't make it? Do we love him any less? Do we think less of him? Of course not. We give him a safe place to land. We praise him for taking the risk and—because baseball is his dream—we remind him that Michael Jordan was cut from his high school basketball team and we encourage him to practice harder and try again.

Why do we tell ourselves any different?

Reason Three: We Convince Ourselves that Failure is Fatal

In Walk #28, I shared the spectacular failure that was our first business, the Rover Group. A quick refresher: we quit great jobs, started a business making pet products, lost everything, borrowed money from friends and family, and lost that too. We almost lost our house and we definitely lost a whole lotta' self-confidence.

But. It wasn't fatal. It was hard, but it wasn't fatal and now, with the benefit of years of hindsight, the lessons we learned were invaluable.

In all likelihood, the risk of failing from taking on a new challenge or setting a new goal for yourself wouldn't be fatal either. So if fear is holding you back, spend some time on your walk really, truly considering what would happen if you failed. Let your mind go to realistic worst-case scenarios. If you enroll in school to earn the degree and you don't finish? If you start another weight loss plan and don't lose any weight? If you start the book you've always dreamed of writing and don't finish it? If you move to Mexico, or decide to spend a year in an RV, or go back to school?

What's your dream and what is the true downside risk of trying it and not succeeding?

It is easy for people to tell you to take chances and risk failure. People tell me that all the time. Heck, I tell other people that all the time. But the risk of failing is scary. Really scary. But it is less scary if you realize what it is you are really scared of—discovering you're not good enough, other people's judgment, being embarrassed, or a catastrophe that is really unlikely to happen. Don't shy away from facing those fears. Instead, stare them dead in the face and then chase your dream anyway.

On today's walk, think about what it is about failure that scares you the most.

● ● ●

Walk # 73: Five Pages: A Fact and a Metaphor

My flight was delayed and I was killing time in the airport bookstore when I spotted a book that had been recommended by a friend. I pulled it off the shelf. It looked like a short read, something I could get through on my flight to California if I ever managed to get on the plane. Excited, I bought the book and began to read it while I continued to wait for the fog to lift and the plane to board.

One of the ideas the author suggested was to read five pages of a book that has the potential to make your life better each day. Now, I love to read and have often said that one of the few things I miss from my days before I had kids to raise and a business to run is the hours I used to spend on a Sunday afternoon, in front of a fire, beneath a blanket, reading. I used to read everything. The entire Sunday edition of the New York Times. Historic novels and biographies, and contemporary novels and mysteries. Books about business and mindfulness and leadership. Books set in Venice and Greece and China. I even worked my way through the first seven letters of the Encyclopedia Britannica before the Internet was a thing.

Alas, my life—at least for the past fifteen years—hasn't allowed for that luxury of time. Instead, I have grabbed my news from a news feed on my phone, surrendered the hope of reading novels, and got most of my business insights and inspiration from magazines and blog posts that I could consume in mini-bites. There was simply no time to become immersed in a great book, so I barely bothered to try.

That day, waiting for the long-delayed flight to board, I decided to heed the author's suggestion and I committed to reading five pages—just five pages—every morning before I start my day. Since then, I get up before my kids and put a fence around thirty morning minutes. I drink coffee, and, as part of my morning routine, read five pages of whatever book I am working my way through at that moment. Even if the book is great and had captured my imagination and attention, I read only five pages. It usually takes me no more than ten or fifteen minutes and I always take notes on things that resonate or that I find particularly interesting or that I want to remember—a habit picked up in law school.

Since I started this practice three years ago, I have read twenty-eight books on subjects including leadership, fitness, how to live a clutter-free life, the life and friendship of the Dalai Lama and Desmond Tutu, how Damon John "rises and grinds" every day, how to design your life in the way that is uniquely yours, and so, so many more.

Twenty-eight books. Five pages at a time.

The metaphor is so obvious I'm not even sure you can call it a metaphor: small steps, taken consistently, yield tremendous results. If you are in sales, making two more sales calls every day will add up to more than 500 additional calls a year. If you save just $5 a day, you will have $1,825 at the end of the year and if you put that money away, in thirty years you could have well over $100,000.

On today's walk, think about one place in your life where you can make a small change that, done consistently and over time, will lead to big results.

● ● ●

Walk # 74: Play is Mission Critical

A few years ago, we added a puppy to our pack. He was eight pounds of puppy love and we named him "Moose". The exuberance, energy, and joy that little bundle of fur invested in each day was a marvel. Puppies play all the time. At least, when they aren't sleeping.

As parents, we recognize how important play is for our kids. It is how they learn, have fun, blow off steam, and develop skills.

As adults, we don't play enough.

Why don't we play more? Because society tells us that play is wasteful and that we should be spending time on more productive pursuits. Schools have scheduled test prep in lieu of recess and converted after school sports into the competitive pursuit of medals and college scholarships. Businesses focus on the output and lose sight of the fun. And we have packed our days with obligations, overloaded our to-do lists, and overcommitted ourselves.

Many of us have simply forgotten what play looks and feels like. Play is the stuff we do because we want to. Not the myriad of things we do that are a "means to an end" but the things we do just because we want to. Play is the act of doing something fun, just for the sake of fun. Play doesn't check anything off your list and, at least on paper, doesn't look like it is helping you achieve your goals.

But it is. A growing body of research is proving that play is mission-critical. Play is critical to creativity and critical thinking. According to research cited in *Essentialism* by Greg McKeown, play: (1) broadens the array of options we see when we confront a situation, (2) is a proven antidote to stress, and (3) has a positive impact on our brain's executive functions—those parts of our brain that enable us to plan, prioritize, schedule, delegate, and make decisions.

Besides, play is fun. And we are entitled to some fun in our lives.

The first step is figuring out what play looks like for you and making time for it. Me? I play on a ski slope, in an ocean, on a hiking trail, or in front of a chessboard with my son.

For you, play is probably something different. Perhaps you play by painting, gardening, or running marathons. Maybe play looks like going to the theater, spending an afternoon in a museum, or having a water balloon fight with your five-year-old. It could be that for you, play is exploring a European city or reading a book in the hammock in your backyard.

There are two kinds of play: planned play and spontaneous play. You need both in your life.

Planned play is play that you need to prioritize and schedule in advance. You have to buy those theater tickets and hire a babysitter. You need to schedule the time off and begin saving now for a future vacation. Planned play is important and requires that you prioritize those bigger goals, dreams, and desires.

Here's a conversation that has played out (no pun intended) in my house so many times over the years that I can barely count them.

Me: I'm so burned out, I've been working so hard, I need a few days to do something fun.

Husband: (because he's awesome) You should plan something.

Me: I'm just too busy. I can't take time off right now.

Husband: So plan something for a few months from now, just do it and put it on your calendar.

Me: But I'm burned out *now* (likely delivered with a little bit of a whine on the now).

Husband: Well, chances are pretty good that you'll need the time then too, so you just need to plan it.

He's right. Time off, vacations, adventures... those things need to be prioritized and planned.

Spontaneous play uses opportunities that arise during the course of the day. When a friend calls and says, "Let's go paddle boarding" or your five-year-old asks, "Mommy, can we go to the park?" and instead of sitting on the bench watching, you swing on the swings beside him. They are the days when school is canceled and instead of railing against the universe about all you had planned to do that day, you bundle up and build a snowman with your kids. They are the times when you say "yes" instead of "no" even when there are jobs to be done, dishes to be washed, and deadlines to be met.

You need both of these kinds of play in your life.

On today's walk, think about how you like to play. And then for the coming week, commit to playing more and notice if it makes you happier, more relaxed, and, ultimately, more productive.

Walk # 75: Too Many Flavors of Jam. Or, One Reason We Don't Get Started

One Saturday in 2000, two researchers set up a tasting at an upscale grocery store in which they displayed, and invited consumers to try, six different flavors of jam. The following Saturday, they set up a tasting booth at the same store but instead of six flavors, they displayed 24 different flavors of jam for customers to try.

The results were fascinating. While significantly more people stopped to check out the display of 24 jams, far fewer of them actually made a purchase than those who only had six flavors to choose from. This research, which has become widely known as the "Jam Study," suggest that, though people are enticed by more choice and options, when confronted with too much choice, they simply don't want to—or can't—make a decision.

Why? Too many choices short-circuit our brain. We become afraid of making the wrong choice and begin to question if we really need a new jam in the first place. This probably doesn't come as a surprise if you stop to consider your own behavior under similar circumstances. We have all experienced the paralysis of choice.

What in the world does this have to do with your goals your dreams? When we think about our goals, our dreams, and our better life, it is easy to become overwhelmed by choices and options. Which path will make me happy? What is the best use of my limited time?

Despite what our culture tells us, most of us don't have one single overriding passion or a simple north star. Few of us have felt that there is one thing that we've been destined to do. If we don't know for sure that our passion is becoming a nurse, writing a book, painting a still life, or starting a business, how is it possible to choose which choice to make and which dream to chase?

Even worse, it is impossible to know with certainty which life will make you happy until you are living it. We become paralyzed with the options, afraid to choose the wrong one. It's no wonder that most of us find ourselves unable to set a goal and reach it. There are too many jams.

There is a very simple solution to this: just choose.

We need to stop being so anxious about choosing a goal. We need to silence the voices that say, "But wait, maybe I should be doing something else" or "What if I invest all this time in this and it turns out it doesn't make me happy?"

They call them risks for a reason—they might not work out. They might not make you happy. But if you let yourself stand in the jam aisle, overwhelmed by the options, until you convince yourself that the jam you have been buying for years is good enough and walk away, you'll continue to eat the same jam for the rest of your life.

So, I ask again: what do you really want? What is the challenge you want to face or the goal you want to reach?

On today's walk, think about the many paths you can take and the many goals you can chase. Picture yourself working toward each one of them and then imagine yourself achieving it. When you get back, write down one goal you are going to work toward, starting today.

Walk # 76: How to Make a Big Decision: A Six-Point Plan

No one can obsess over a decision like I can. No one. Big or small, my mind can churn for hours on all of the "should I's," "shouldn't I's," and "what ifs." I want to look at every issue and explore every possible ramification. I want to get it right. It can be debilitating and prevent me from moving forward. Over the years, I've figured out a very specific strategy to help work through all kinds of decisions.

Before I begin trying to make the decision, I remind myself that the decisions that I think are monumental probably aren't. Because we can rarely predict which decisions will ultimately be the most important—it could be walking left instead of right—turn right and meet the man of your dreams, turn left and get hit by a bus. Chances are that the decision you think is the most important decision of your life probably isn't. That said, decisions still need to be made. Here's my tried and true six-step process to help you walk through those big—and little—decisions.

Step one: identify all of your options. Get creative here. Even ideas that might seem farfetched may lead you to other ideas. Since we know that walking fuels creativity, taking a long walk and freeing your mind to ponder all of the options is an excellent way to begin to process an important decision.

Step two: educate yourself. Be sure that you have all of the information you need to make your decision. When Eric and I were first trying to decide whether or not to quit our corporate jobs and head out on an entrepreneurial path, one of the pieces of data we needed was real clarity on exactly how much income we needed to support ourselves and how long our savings would last before we needed our new business to be profitable.

Step three: break out the old pro and con list. Grab a piece of paper, make a line down the center and list the pros on one side and the cons on the other. Don't edit your thoughts, just capture every pro and con that comes to mind. Keep in mind that the sheer number of items in each column shouldn't decide it for you because some things will be more important than others.

Step four: remember your priorities. As you evaluate the pros and cons, deliberately consider the things that are most important to you. Even if something is very tempting, it might not align with the things that are most important to you. If being home to get your kids off the bus is extremely important to you, that new job might not align with your priorities—even if it means a raise.

Step five: step outside yourself. Sometimes it is hard to be objective about a big decision that may significantly impact our lives. One way to get a bit of that objectivity is to pretend that you are offering advice to a friend who is wrestling with the decision. What questions would you ask and what advice would you give your best friend? If you can enlist someone to playact with you, even better. If not, play out the conversation in your mind as if you were talking to someone else.

Step six: flip a coin. Simply assign an option to each side of the coin, give it a flip and look at the result. If your gut says "yay" then you know that is the right decision. But if the result of the coin toss makes your gut say "yikes" or you feel a tingle of disappointment, then you know what you want to do—and it's not what the coin toss dictated. The coin toss is often the best way to tune in that all-important "gut check."

On today's walk, think about a decision you've been wrestling with or putting off and really dig into it, putting it through this six-step process. If it helps, you can write these six steps down on a piece of paper so that you can really work through them one by one.

Walk # 77: Abundance vs. Scarcity

In 1845, a fungus infested the potato crops of Ireland and set the Irish Potato Famine in motion. The famine lasted for seven years during which millions died from hunger and malnutrition. Without potatoes, there simply wasn't enough food to go around. The Irish people were living in a time of tragic scarcity.

If you are reading this book, you are likely living in a world where there is plenty of food, water, and opportunity to go around. A world in which you do not need to hoard your potatoes to be sure that your children have enough to eat. Where their success does not mean your failure, their new car doesn't mean you can't have one too and their accomplishments do not make it any less likely that you will achieve your goals. Yet so many of us continue to feel like we live in a world of scarce resources, where another's success means our failure.

Living with a feeling of scarcity makes us believe there is a limited amount of success to go around. We look upon the success of others with envy and resentment because we believe their success somehow diminishes our ability to succeed. And if you believe this, then it's no wonder another's success makes you feel envious and resentful, thinking "How did she get so lucky?" We resent the success of others because it makes us feel like their success makes our success less likely.

Nothing could be further from the truth. Being surrounded by people who are achieving success doesn't diminish the likelihood of your success. To the contrary, there's a ton of research that shows that surrounding yourself with successful people can actually improve the likelihood of your success.

Moreover, living with a spirit of abundance in and of itself raises the likelihood of your success. Why? Because people who are living with a spirit of generosity are open and expansive and, frankly, happier. When you support others and cheer for their successes, chances are that they will cheer you on in turn.

Scarcity is closely aligned to fear, and I get that. If you see someone around you who has achieved a major goal or brought about real change, chances are good that makes you feel afraid that you will not have success. Let me give you a super practical example. Imagine that you and a friend are each wrestling with your weight and each one of you has about fifty pounds to lose. Together, you embark on a health and wellness journey. Together, you commit to keeping a food diary, eating more fresh fruits and vegetables, walking at least two miles each day, and avoiding the dangerous post-dinner sweet snacks. Fast forward three months later and your friend has lost fifteen pounds and you've lost four. Jealous? Of course. Frustrated? Absolutely. Angry? Possibly. Sad? Most likely.

Now you have two choices. You can look at her success with frustration and beat yourself up for the walks you skipped and the desserts you indulged in. You can blame your kids or your partner. You can make excuses. You can give up.

Or you can celebrate your friend's success with a genuine spirit, use her success to inspire your own, learn her tricks and tactics, and realize that if she did it, so can you. Like so many of the lessons toward living a better life, the choice to live with a spirit of abundance is largely a function of sheer force of will.

On today's walk think about the last time you felt envious, angry, or resentful at another's success. As you walk, bring that person to mind and intentionally think:

- I am happy for them.
- There is plenty to go around and their success means I'm more likely to achieve success.
- What are the lessons I can learn from them?

Walk # 78: Don't Slow Down at the Finish Line

For five years, I studied Shotokan karate. My sensei was an incredibly strong German woman who sported a blond ponytail and could take you with a sharp word or a single roundhouse kick. But step outside of her karate uniform and second-degree black belt and she was warm, funny, and approachable. We became friends and would sometimes talk about her business.

"When do you tend to lose students?" I asked one day.

"Either within the first six months after they start," she said, "or when they are brown belts."

Brown belt is the last step before black belt. And earning a black belt in karate is a big deal. It means you have achieved a level of mastery over the Shotokan basics. It is a badge of honor and, though it doesn't mean your training is "complete," it is a tremendous accomplishment.

"That doesn't make any sense at all," I said. "People quit right before they've earned their black belt?" I was incredulous. The years and years of hard work it takes to earn a brown belt and then, with the ultimate prize in sight, people walk away? That's when they quit? It made no sense to me.

Until I achieved my brown belt. And then quit.

Now, I had all kinds of excuses. There was a new sensei teaching some of the classes whom I didn't like. I was busy with work and kids and I didn't have time to go to class three days a week. I was bored and wanted to try something different. Maybe I just didn't want it badly enough.

Or maybe there was something deeper and more insidious at work.

In *The Big Leap: Conquer Your Hidden Fear and Take Life to the Next Level*, author Gay Hendricks theorizes that we all face what he calls an "upper limit problem." He believes that each of us has a level of success that feels comfortable and that when we reach that upper limit, we will self-sabotage to stay there without even realizing we are doing it. I know, that seems crazy right? We get close to a goal, or we finally begin to make progress and then we lose momentum. We backslide. We give up. We regain five pounds, turn in a project late, or take our foot off the gas at work.

Many of us have a tendency to slow down before the finish line or quit right before we reach the next level, even though that is precisely the moment when we need to speed up, double down, and raise the intensity. Why do we sometimes get so close and then take our foot off of the gas? Why did I complete sixty-three chapters of this book and almost walk away?

Each of us has an identity comprised of what we show the world and what we tell ourselves. Most of us have become comfortable with that identity. Even if we want to change it, improve it, or "level up," changing our status quo conflicts with that identity and on some deep and likely unconscious level, there is part of us that is afraid—or at the very least reluctant—to bring about real change that might change that identity.

Okay, it is also hard. The work needed to progress from brown belt to black is hard. It takes time, commitment, and work.

And so we slow down just before we cross the threshold into the unknown.

On today's walk, think about times in your life when you have quit before your black belt. Times you have taken the first steps toward making an enduring change in your life or accomplishing something meaningful. And, while we try not to look backward, for today, really think about how your life might have changed and ask yourself, with honesty, what fears might have held you back.

Then think about the path you are walking right now and the goals and dreams you have for your life. Allow yourself to look at what your life will look like when you achieve those goals and realize that dream. Do you feel a tingle of fear along with a tingle of excitement? Some say if your dreams don't scare you, they aren't big enough. I'm not entirely sure that's true, but I do believe that if your dreams scare you, even a tiny bit, you need to recognize and acknowledge those fears because it is the only way to accelerate and blow across the finish line.

Walk # 79: Squirrel

"I think I've ruined my brain." Eric and I were sitting outside on the deck late one afternoon.

"What do you mean?" he asked.

"It's so hard to hold a single thought, to focus on one thing. It's like my brain is constantly bouncing in different directions all the time."

And then, like he was being paid to do it, a squirrel ran across the yard in front of us. Our dog Moose, who had been lying quietly at my feet, bolted to action and sprinted across the yard.

"Squirrel," I said, following him with my eyes. No matter what Moose is doing, a squirrel cannot be ignored. It must be chased.

And that is how I find my mind these days, with squirrels presenting themselves in the form of emails, text messages, Facebook messages, and the opportunity to instantly seek the answer to any question that crosses my mind. Hmmm, I wonder what the weather will be like today. Hmmm, I wonder if Melissa had her baby. Hmmm, I wonder if all dogs chase squirrels or just mine.

We've become so proficient at moving quickly from one thing to another that we've sacrificed our ability for deep and meaningful thought. Our reduced attention span has been well documented. In an oft-cited study from Microsoft, the average person has an attention span of eight seconds—which, researchers say, is less than that of a goldfish.

I believe it. Before the advent of social media, back when I used to write first drafts by hand on a long legal pad rather than on the computer, I had a reliable three-hour attention span. I could dig deep into a project, focus intently, and do my best work for three hours after which my brain was tired and I needed a break. But wow, the work I could produce during those three hours.

These days, tapping into that place of genuine focus and deep work is far more challenging.

First, there are all of the added responsibilities of my life. In the days of the three-hour attention span, I could wake up early in the morning, go out for a three-mile run, stop at my favorite coffee shop on the way back to my apartment, and settle in for an uninterrupted three-hour writing session. These days, my mornings are far different. Wake up. Do my morning Goalpost routine. Empty the dishwasher, make my daughter's lunch, let the dog out, wake the kids, chat with them before bus comes, do the morning dishes, and text my dad. That's a whole lotta' distraction and I haven't even opened my computer.

Second, there are all of the things that ring and ping and demand our attention and we jump whenever we hear a ding or ping. In fact, as I was writing this very section, I received a text from my BFF. I tried to fight the urge to look, but I lost. "Up for a catch-up chat?" She asked. "Sure," I replied, and put this section away for the fifteen minutes she and I were talking and then the twenty minutes it took me to get back into the writing flow.

Third, we have retrained our brains to crave the quick hit. We consume bite-sized bits of news and information. We read for less than a minute. We scroll through social media feeds barely registering 90% of what we see. In this way, we have taught our brains to crave the quick hit.

Finally, many of us live our professional lives on temptation island. The computer on which we work offers up all measures of distraction all the time. Looking at my screen right now, there are five tabs open across the top and 26 icons just below the words I am typing. When I hit a block in my thinking it is oh so easy to simply look away. Or think, "Maybe there's some research I haven't seen on this topic that I should look at" or "I wonder how much engagement yesterday's video got."

Squirrel.

So what are we to do? Is it possible to rebuild our attention and increase our focus in this always-on, hyper-connected, overscheduled, constantly pinging world?

The most recent brain research suggests that our brains form new neural pathways throughout our lives. That means you absolutely, positively can retrain your brain for better focus. Here are seven ways to do that.

First, recognize that your ability to focus is a muscle you can strengthen. Force yourself to focus. When you are working on a project and you find yourself tempted to click over to social media or hop into your email, acknowledge the urge and gently bring your mind back to the task at hand. Recognize the pull of the distraction and deliberately resist it. Over time, this will help to strengthen your focus.

Second, create as distraction-free of an environment as possible. What this looks like will be different for everyone. For some people who work at home, it might mean getting a babysitter and heading to a local coffee shop away from the distraction of laundry, dishes, bills, and other household chores. For others, it might mean silencing all of those pesky notifications and closing your email. Still others might seek the quiet of a library. When I was practicing law and had an important brief to write, I would take over a small conference room, pile books and blank legal pads on the table, and close the door for, you guessed it, three hours. No phones, no distractions, and no other projects calling my attention.

Third, nurture habits that foster concentration. For instance, if you are striving to concentrate on writing, set aside a specific time of day and create rituals around it. Decide that you will write each day between 6:00 and 8:00 am, after you fix yourself a cup of tea, put on your favorite writing sweatshirt, and queue up some Chopin or Beyoncé in the background. Same routine, every day.

Fourth, build up. I want to build back up to three hours. I'm starting with the Pomodoro technique, a productivity technique developed in the early 90s by author Francesco Cirillo. The approach is simple: set a timer and focus for 50 minutes. When the timer goes off, take a ten-minute break. If even fifty minutes feels like an eternity, begin to strengthen your focus muscle by reading slightly longer articles, books, and stories. Set a ten-minute focus timer. Tomorrow, set your timer for eleven minutes.

Fifth, have an easy way to capture distracting thoughts as they come to you. When a thought pops into your brain, your mind will sometimes continue to ruminate on it, especially if it is something you are afraid you might forget. Have a handy place to capture the thought or the idea. For me, whenever I'm working, I have an open notebook and a pen right beside the computer. If a thought that seems important pops into my mind, I capture it in my notebook and quickly go back to what I'm doing. The key is not to act on every thought, idea, or task that pops into your brain, but to simply capture it for later.

Sixth, meditate. Yup, here we go again. Mediation is a form of exercise for your mind. As we've talked about before, do it even when you don't feel like it. Do it even if you think you are bad at it. Do it because, over time, it is one of the very best ways to strengthen your focus muscle.

And, finally, one of the first and best things you can do is... well... walk. Taking a 30-minute walk away from your computer and the competing responsibilities of your home or office is an ideal way to begin to rebuild your focus. Research shows that exercise improves focus for several hours even after the walk has been completed.

On today's walk, think about how you have been training your brain to jump from task to task and decide to begin working to improve your ability to focus.

Walk # 80: Embrace the Suck

To get where you want to go, achieve the things you want to achieve, and make meaningful change in your life requires work. Always.

Most of us underestimate just how much work it takes to get where we want to go. There are two reasons for this. First, the people who are already there rarely share the work it took to get there. Okay, there are the occasional unicorns who were born with perfect abs and perfect hair, but I promise you, they are few and far between. Second, if we really, truly accepted how hard it would be, we would rarely even start.

Meaningful accomplishments require a boatload of work. Often that work is not pretty, it's not glamorous, and more often than not, it's not fun. Satisfying? Yes. Soul inspiring? Maybe. Exciting? Sometimes. But hard. How do you get through it? To borrow an expression from the military: embrace the suck.

Yup, the only way you will effectuate meaningful change in your life will be to embrace the suck. Because you've been doing the things you want to do. You've been eating the foods you want to eat. You've been reading the things you feel like reading. You've been watching the TV whenever you feel like it. All of your current habits have gotten you to the exact situation you are in right now. But if you are reading this book, that means there are aspects of your life you'd like to change or improve. Those changes will take work, no matter what they are.

That work might suck.

Let's talk about exercise because it is the clearest example. I was at the barn yesterday, the place where I do CrossFit-inspired workouts with five other women. These workouts usually last two hours and they are hard. Really hard. We lift heavy things, we run, bike, or row, and then we lift heavy things again. We climb ropes, jump over boxes, throw medicine balls against the wall, and we do more burpees than I can count. It is hard, grueling work. The women in the barn are a mixed bag: a former dancer, three moms, one police officer, and two entrepreneurs. When a new woman joined the barn, "Wow," she said after the first workout. "You guys don't mess around."

"I know," I said. "These girls are tough." Then the conversation turned to why we do what we do.

"I work out this hard so that I can do my job. And so I can eat," the police officer said.

"I do it so I can chase my kids," a mom of two offered.

"I do it because I love feeling strong," the other entrepreneur said.

"I just love it," I added.

But as I reflected on why I work out, and why I work out hard, I realized that's not entirely true. The work is hard. It hurts. Most days, I feel like a failure since, as the oldest member of this barn crew, I am usually the slowest and the weakest, lifting lighter weights, and finishing behind everyone else. The workouts usually suck. So why do I keep going?

Because I love how I feel when I'm done. Because I love the feeling of getting stronger. Because when I started, I could not do a single pull-up and now I can do seven without stopping and 25 if I take breaks between them. Because at 50, I learned to climb a rope. Because I work with a group of women who tell me I'm doing great and mean it, even when I'm 30 seconds behind them.

The actual work sucks. So if you think that losing weight, getting strong, writing a book, earning a new degree, getting a new job, painting your bathroom, or learning to climb a rope is going to be easy, well, it's not. It is going to be work. And at times that work is going to suck. And the only way to get there is to embrace the suck.

What does that mean? It means you accept that it is going to be hard. Accept that you will be challenged. Accept that you will have failure along the way. Accept that you will feel like quitting.

And then you need to *not* quit. You need to smile through the suck. You need to recognize and celebrate the small victories. You need to rely on your pack to tell you that you are doing a good job. You need to embrace the suck and keep going. Frankly, it's that simple.

On today's walk, think about how much work you need to do to achieve what you want, and then decide—really decide—if you are willing to do the work. If not, that's okay. Maybe this is not the perfect time for you to chase a big dream or reach for a big goal. But if it is, accept that you are going to have to embrace the suck along the way.

● ● ●

Walk # 81: What?

When I was little, I asked a lot of questions. Like... a lot of questions. It made my mother crazy because I would keep asking and digging until she would ultimately throw up her hands in frustration, *"I don't know why the sky is blue, where we come from, or what the meaning of life is."* I wasn't trying to annoy or frustrate her, I just had an insatiable appetite to understand the world around me.

I don't believe I'm alone in that. I believe that we all come to this life with a desire to understand the "why" and the "how" and the "what for." Over time, when we realize that some of the biggest questions are going to remain unanswered no matter how much we crave understanding, we begin to give up asking. Then we go to school. A place where we are supposed to be encouraged to ask questions, take chances, and make mistakes. Sadly, that natural curiosity is rarely fed in traditional schools.

Then we become adults who head off into the workplace where we are supposed to have answers, not questions. We don't want to embarrass ourselves by asking a question we think we are supposed to know the answer to. We don't want to reveal ignorance or ineptitude. We don't want to look stupid.

Finally, we become parents, and at that point, we believe that we are supposed to have the answers. But we don't. Years ago I was floating in a pool in Jamaica alongside my friend Sandy. She'd had her two kids young, and now, in her mid-30s, she found herself mother to teenagers. She had just gotten off a call with her daughter. "I'm too young to have teenagers," she said, floating on her back. "They expect me to have all of the answers when I barely know anything myself."

When did it become a badge of honor to pretend that we have the answers? Here is the truth: the only way you are going to get where you want to go is by being willing to ask questions. Lots of questions.

The exciting thing is that we have never had so much wisdom and information at our fingertips. The Internet is literally bursting with free knowledge on just about every subject imaginable. So start there and educate yourself as best as you possibly can.

Once you have a basic understanding of whatever it is you are trying to answer or learn, begin to ask questions of real, live people. You will undoubtedly discover that most people are incredibly generous with their wisdom. As human beings, we are hard-wired to want to help others. In fact, as we talked about during Walk #60, people will actually like you *more* if you ask for their help. The trick is asking smart questions (which is why you need to do your research first), and then really listening to the answers.

Drop the belief that you are supposed to have all of the answers and reconnect with your childlike curiosity. Ask questions, seek answers.

On today's walk, think about one thing you are hoping to accomplish and identify some of the questions you will need to have answered.

● ● ●

Walk # 82: Stand on Your Head

I love to stand on my head. I know that's a weird thing for a woman in her fifties to say, but I do. I love how standing on my head engages my entire body to maintain my balance and I love feeling strong and straight and balanced. I stand on my head at the beach, in parks, at the gym, and pretty much anywhere else where I can put something soft beneath my head. But what I love most is the way standing on my head delivers a different perspective of familiar things.

We all have our patterns, habits, and ruts. We fix our coffee the same way each day, take the same route to work, and often repeat the same conversations with our kids, partners, and friends. We love our habits and patterns.

But there are downsides to these comfortable routines: they reduce our ability to think creatively, experience new things, and have fun. It is such a paradox: we crave comfort, stability, and predictability, yet we get the most joy, have the most fun, and form the deepest memories from experiences outside of our usual routine.

In order to create the richest life experience you can, you have to find ways to get different perspectives and see things with fresh eyes. Find moments to stand on your head.

Shoshin is a word in Zen Buddhism that encourages people to approach life with a "beginner's mind." And while the meaning is layered and complex, it is also simple. Shoshin suggests that we strive to approach things—even things that are familiar—with a beginner's mind, as if we are seeing it, learning it, or experiencing it for the first time. Shoshin reminds us to let go of our preconceptions and cultivate an open mind.

Like most things in Zen Buddhism, this is much harder than it sounds. We tend to look at things the same way and do things the same way, often without stopping to ask ourselves why. And then, we stop seeing them. We go through the motions and replicate our old ways of doing things over and over again. When I stand on my head, it immediately flips the switch, changes my perspective, and forces me to look at things with fresh eyes.

So next time you are facing a challenge, working on a problem, or realize that you have been walking through your days on auto-pilot, find a way to stop and stand on your head. Fix your coffee in a different way. Take a different route to work. Climb up on to a bench to look out over your backyard. Eat breakfast for dinner. Spend a full day without your phone.

If you are like most of us, you often walk the same trails, paths, or neighborhoods. On today's walk, strive to see that walk with a beginner's mind, as if you've never been there before.

● ● ●

Walk # 83: Look for the Open Spaces

After college, Eric taught skiing in Colorado for three winters while he figured out what he wanted to do with his life. One of his favorite stories is about a group lesson with a bunch of eight-year-olds on a snowy Saturday. Just before lunch, Eric led the group to the top of a big, open trail. It would be challenging for them, but not beyond their abilities. Most of the group took off, whooping and hollering as eight-year-olds are known to do while skiing.

But one boy hung back, staring down the snow-covered hill. He wasn't moving.

"Are you ready?" Eric asked.

"But what about the tree?" the boy replied with trepidation. Eric looked down to where the kid was pointing and sure enough, in the middle of a big, wide-open field was a single small tree. "What if I hit it?" the boy asked nervously.

"There is plenty of space all around it," Eric said. "Just look at the open spaces and you'll ski right past it."

Eric waited at the top and watched as the kid began skiing cautiously down the trail. As he skied, Eric could see him constantly turning his head to the left to glance at the tree. The more he looked at it, the closer he got to it. The closer he got to it, the more he stared at it until, yup, the kid hit the tree.

Eric skied down quickly to where the kid was laying in the snow. Unhurt, the boy was nevertheless upset. "You see," he said crying, "I told you I was going to hit the tree."

Since that day, Eric has adopted an expression which has become part of the lexicon of our relationship: "Look for the open spaces, don't focus on the tree."

This metaphor applies to pretty much every aspect of our lives. If you focus on the negative, you will be pulled toward the negative. If you focus on the faults, you will be pulled toward the faults. Every single day, there will be things that don't go your way. And every day, you have the opportunity to focus on the things that didn't go your way, or focus on the things that did. What you see is what you get, so keep the trees in your peripheral vision and look for the open spaces.

It is easy to criticize an idea, find fault with a plan, or call out potential pitfalls and problems. When encountering a new idea, it is almost reflexive to say, "That won't work because..." What is far more difficult is to see the issues but then go the step further to identify the open spaces, the solutions, or the path around the tree. Here are three things that help.

Practice gratitude.

We talked during Walk #47 about the almost magical properties of a meaningful gratitude practice. Maintaining a gratitude practice has been shown to train your mind to focus on the positive and the good. But for it to work, it has to be a regular, ongoing, and consistent practice. So every morning, I make an entry in my gratitude journal and I identify something I'm grateful for. Some days, I find that I am profoundly grateful for the people in my life, the family I love, the friends who support me, the business I am so fortunate to steward, my health, my strength, or my parents. Other days, the best I can come up with is being grateful for a hot cup of coffee or the chance to try again. But I begin every day by turning my focus to at least one thing for which I am grateful.

Count the wins. Even the small ones. Especially the small ones.

I end every day with a long list of things still undone. My to-do list is long and my goals are tremendous. It is very, very easy—and tempting—to end the day thinking about the things that were left undone or that didn't go well.

So, I recently added a new practice to my life. Each night, I capture a win from the day. I identify something that did go my way, some small success and I also identify something I accomplished that I feel good about, proud of, or which I believe was at least one step in the right direction of my dreams.

Learn the power of the word yet.

In Walk #31, we talked about the power of yet, and about how powerful it is to simply add the word "yet" to the end of any thought that reflects something you want to become or accomplish. Simply adding the word yet takes your eye off the tree and into the open spaces.

"I'm not a published author, yet."

Yes, you do need to know where the trees are. You need to spot the roadblocks, potential problems, and pitfalls. You can't ignore them. But once you see them and identify them, then you have to look for the open spaces.

If you focus on the problems, challenges and pitfalls—if you stare at them—you will inevitably navigate toward them.

When the inevitable trees pop up in the middle of your path, take a good look at them, consider their size and shape and where they are positioned. And then look for the open spaces. The solution. The positives. The things for which you are grateful. The open space beside them. Ski there. It is really that simple.

On today's walk, think about your tendency to focus on the trees and make a decision to shift your attention to the open spaces.

● ● ●

Walk # 84: Little Things Matter

Years ago, there was a popular book called *Don't Sweat the Small Stuff, and It's All Small Stuff* by Richard Carlson. The theme was that the majority of the things we spend our time fretting over, being upset about, or angry about don't matter in the long run. The guy who stole your spot in the parking lot at the mall the week before Christmas? Being late for a dinner reservation? The "C" your teenager brought home in Spanish? The mess that is your mudroom? None of it matters.

Viewed through a certain lens, it is true. As we've talked about, in 100 years, all new people. We will all live, grow, and die. The things that we spend most of our time worrying about won't matter.

But the little things do. In fact, the little things are the most important things.

My son, who somehow morphed overnight from a tiny little bundle that fit in the crook of my arm to a fully-formed eighteen-year-old with opinions and body hair, will be leaving for college in a few short months. When I reflect on his early childhood, I vividly remember a single night-time feeding. It was early spring. I had recovered from the emergency c-section that brought him to this world and I was feeling good. I had slept three or four hours before I heard his telling "I'm hungry" cry. I crept into his room, picked him up, and together we settled into the nursing chair. The house seemed preternaturally quiet and as I nurtured this tiny being whom I loved so fiercely, I thought, "I want to remember this moment, this feeling, for the rest of my life." And I do. I don't remember the thousand other feedings. I barely remember the endless sleepless nights. But I do remember every detail of that one quiet night.

The little moments matter. In fact, the little moments are everything. Do not let those moments sail past you. Grab them. Notice them and cherish them.

Not only do the little moments matter for the sake of their own magical moments, they also stack up to create the big wins and the big goals. Every goal that gets completed is the result of a thousand tiny goals. Every big win is the consequence of a thousand small wins. Often, we let those tiny goals and small wins go by unnoticed. Uncelebrated. And we tell ourselves that the small things don't matter. But they do.

Your success will be achieved only as the result of a million small steps that you take consistently over time. If you want to lose weight, you need to make a million small choices: choose water over juice, walking over riding, apples over cookies. You need to commit to those daily walks and say no to that glass of wine. If you want to earn a degree to open a new professional door, you need to take a million small steps. Apply instead of procrastinating. Attend class rather than play hooky. Turn in the paper on time instead of late. If you want to start or grow your business, you need to work instead of scrolling social media. You need to get up earlier rather than sleep in later.

The great news is that because your success in all things will be the result of a thousand small actions, that means if you screw up—and you will—that one screw up will have virtually no impact on your success. None. You have a thousand chances to do better. The problem we run into is when we tell ourselves that since we screwed up, we should give up. Few places is this truer than when you are trying to lose weight. But let me be really clear here: one cookie, one slice of birthday cake, or one skipped walk will have zero impact on any long term weight loss or fitness goal. But if you tell yourself, "Well, I've blown it now," and let one screw up give you permission to quit, well, then it is game over.

The beauty is that the little things matter because they add up to big things, but that also means that one little screw up just doesn't matter. So, step one is to realize that the little things do matter. Step two is to realize that when you screw up—and you inevitably will—you have to brush it off and get right back to it.

On today's walk, think about two things. First, recall some beautiful moments in time that are special to you. Replay them and enjoy them. Second, consider any tendency you have to let one misstep derail you.

Walk # 85: Go First

We moved the summer before our son began seventh grade and our daughter third. Though we only moved six miles, we moved to a new town and a new school district. On the first day of school, our daughter went off to third grade, strode into Mr. Kahoffer's class, sat down on the carpet with the other kids, and never looked back.

My son, well that was a different story. He had a wonderful friend group at his old school. He was comfortable there. He knew the teachers, the kids, the families, and where the boys' room was located. He was a kid who liked his routines. He did not want to move, even if it was only six miles.

The town we moved to is a small town in all the best ways and the entire seventh grade was only 70 kids, many of whom had been together since kindergarten.

The first few weeks were a disaster. My sweet and sensitive son came home each day either in tears or so angry that he went directly to his room and slammed the door. Dinners were long as he sent me silent, scathing looks or told me outright that I ruined his life. I've never been entirely sure why his anger was directed mostly at me rather than at both my husband and me, but I took the brunt.

We tried. We invited families with kids in his grade over for BBQs and brunches. We encouraged him to join clubs and teams. It got better, but not by much.

One day, my son came home and, in a rare moment of genuine communication, said, "These kids have all been together since kindergarten. They all have shared memories and I wasn't there for any of it. I never know what they are talking about," he added despondently.

I turned to Eric and said, "Go make him some friggin' memories."

My husband, who is awesome, reached out to the dads of the boys with whom Mason had begun to develop fledgling friendships, the dads from the families who we welcomed for brunch and BBQs. "Let's take the boys on a father-son camping and rafting trip for a weekend this summer," he suggested. And he sold it. *"We only have five summers left before our boys head off to college. It will be great. I'll plan everything.*" The boys' annual summer rafting trip was born. And it changed the entire trajectory of my son's high school experience.

To make this happen, Eric had to be willing to go first. To make an overture to a group of guys he didn't know very well. To be the first to extend a hand, make a suggestion, or, as we like to call it, "drive the bus."

During the course of your days and your life, you will have millions of opportunities to go first. When you see a person in the grocery store who looks like the mom of one of your kid's classmates, you can be the first to say hello. As you are checking out, you can be the first to say good morning to the cashier. When someone in your life is in need, you can be the first to reach out to offer help and support. You can be the person who goes first.

Why? Because going first, taking initiative, and being willing to open the door to new connections opens the door to new opportunities. The idea circles back to when we talked about luck. People make their own luck and one way to do that is by going first. Going first trains you to be proactive, take initiative, and embrace a bias toward action. In order to get the life you want, you can't wait for things to happen to you, you must go out and make them happen.

Going first helps to foster community. Here's a secret: most people are shy. Most people will hang back and wait for someone else to make the first move. Most people are afraid of rejection, making a mistake, or being embarrassed. Most people are unwilling to approach that other mom in the grocery store for fear of being wrong—what if she's not that other mom from Sadie's class? It will be so embarrassing. But what would happen if another mom approached you in the grocery store and said, "Hey, aren't you Mitchell's mom?"

"Nope, not me," you reply.

"Oh, sorry," she says. "Well, have a great day anyway," she offers with a smile before wheeling her cart away.

Now, here's the thing. What would you think of that woman? Would you think less of her for making a mistake or more of her for making the overture? Would her parting "Have a great day anyway" make you feel good or bad? I dare say it would leave you with a smile and make you feel good. There is nothing embarrassing about making a mistake.

Finally, going first simply helps to spread joy in the world. And that in and of itself is immensely valuable.

On today's walk, think about all of the opportunities you have in your life to go first and decide that, at least for today, you will take them.

Walk # 86: Beware Parkinson's Law

We entertain. A lot. Dinner for a dozen people? No sweat. BBQ for 20? Sure. Want to meet at the beach for a bonfire? We'll bring the s'mores.

I'm always the first to say yes because I love filling my home with awesome people. I love the sound of laughter and the clink of wine glasses. If a few weeks have gone by without a group of people in my backyard, I will turn to Eric and say, "Let's host a brunch" or invite friends out for the weekend. Sometimes we'll see if the neighbors are free and we'll throw something on the grill. Pizza party, pool party, or picnic—I'm in.

Invariably, at some point during the afternoon, I will look at Eric and say, "There is *no way* we are going to get everything done before people arrive." Yet somehow, by the time guests arrive at the front door, the house is clean, the wine is chilled, the food is prepped, and I am showered and dressed in something other than the clothes I walked in that morning. And this is the case pretty much no matter how early we begin to prepare—whether we have spent the day getting ready, or rushed home from the office with only an hour to spare. How does this happen? How is it that the same amount of work takes significantly different amounts of time?

The answer is Parkinson's Law. It is human nature to allow work to expand to fill the time available for its completion. The theory is loosely based on an essay from the 1950s about how bureaucracies become less efficient as they grow larger.

Why? First, we often add nonessential tasks to the projects we take on. Over time I've realized that the amount of time we spend preparing for a party has no bearing on its success. A party is not more fun if I managed to sweep under the couch or remembered to light candles in the bathroom. The salmon is only marginally better if it marinated for four hours instead of forty minutes. When we run out of time, we are forced to reduce a task to its most essential elements and skip the other stuff. When you have a task to accomplish, strip it down to its most essential elements and do them first

Second, the "luxury" of more time gives us an excuse to be inefficient. When I was in law school, my fellow students would meet in the library for "study groups." Several months into my first year, I joined one of these groups and met them at the designated table on the first floor of the law library. What followed was three hours of discussion that meandered from topic to topic, occasionally devolved into arguments, and was frequently punctuated by discussions of who was next up to run to the cafeteria for more coffee. By the end, I was exhausted and hadn't learned a thing. Fortunately, exams were not for another two months.

When you get to work, get to work. Set a timeframe. This is challenging because many of the tasks we undertake on our way to accomplishing our goal are not time-bound. Take my quest to master double unders by the end of the year. Nobody cares if I accomplish it by December 31. In order to make it happen, I set a hard and fast deadline for myself: I would link 30 double-unders by the end of the year. Then I broke that down into smaller milestones and wrote them down. The deadlines loom large in my calendar and in my mind.

Now no one else set that deadline for me. If I miss it, no one will notice. But I have drawn a line in the sand. I have created time pressure. On today's walk, think about the tasks and projects that are next on your list, figure out how long it will take you to do them, and set a deadline. Make this your practice.

Walk # 87: Some Days are Harder Than Others

I wake up in the same body, in the same house, beside the same husband, with the same two kids sleeping down the hall, and the same dog sleeping at the foot of my bed. I have the same job. I have the same long, long list of things to do.

So why is it that some days I feel hopeful, positive, and optimistic and other days bored, depressed, and afraid of the future? Why is it that some days I can deadlift 185 pounds and other days 75 pounds destroys me? Why is it that some days I have the energy to take on the world and other days I feel like I'm slogging through quicksand?

We all have those days. We all have fluctuations in our energy and our mood. We've all had our feelings hurt, experienced loss, or just had one of those days. Some of us have bigger swings than others. If the bad days are so bad that you can't get out of bed, well, that's a whole 'nother kettle of fish. You should run—not walk—in the direction of mental health services, support, and help.

But for those of us who have typical good days and not-so-good days, how do you push through a not-so-good day? And how do you refuse to let a not-so-good day ruin a week, a month, a career, or a relationship?

Step one is to recognize the day for what it is. Eric and I will sometimes refer to a crappy day with the shorthand "biorhythms." That is definitely not a technically correct use of that word, but we use it to explain a day when we feel crappy for no particularly good reason. So, if you are feeling down, take a moment to see if you can identify what's bothering you. If it is something specific, a conversation you need to have, a particular stress at work, a worry about a child, not enough exercise, or too much wine, see if you can put your finger on it and address it. If it is just a general down day, see it for what it is.

Step two is to see if you can kick that bad day in the teeth and turn it around. There are four tried and true ways to do this:

Exercise. Get out and take a walk or a run. Hop on a bike. Weed your garden. Whatever floats your boat. Endorphins are the single best way to beat a generally blue day. One caveat: You will NOT feel like doing this. Do it anyway.

Get to work. Find a task that you can complete and force yourself to do it. Take action. Keep moving and working.

Do something for someone else. Boatloads of research and tons of anecdotal evidence shows that doing something kind for someone else can immediately boost your mood.

Spend time with a friend. Better yet, spend time with a friend walking. Nope, you won't feel like doing this either. Do it anyway.

If none of these things work, sometimes you just have to see a day for what it is—a lousy day. Once in a while, you just need to binge-watch crappy television while eating Ben & Jerry's Phish Food.

Here's what not to do.

Don't self-medicate a low energy day with caffeine—you will just set yourself up for a cycle. Don't spend the day on social media looking at how awesome everyone else's life looks (because I promise you, their lives are not as picture-perfect as they look). If possible, avoid making big or important decisions—it is not the day to quit your job or ask your husband for a divorce. Finally, don't let one bad day leak into the next. Ate a huge bowl of ice cream on Tuesday? That is no reason to follow it up with chocolate pie on Wednesday. Skipped your morning routine on Monday? All the more reason to get right back to it on Tuesday. Didn't walk on Friday? Push yourself out the door on Saturday morning. And most importantly, if the number of down days increases or the down keeps getting lower, get professional help.

On today's walk, notice how your walk changes your mood and hold onto that thought to remind yourself, on future down days, of the value of lacing up your sneakers and getting out the door.

● ● ●

Walk # 88: Can You Be Content and Ambitious?

All of my life, I had big dreams, big goals and a deep desire to impact the world in a meaningful way. I believed that to accomplish those things, you could never be satisfied. You always had to be striving for more—more reach, more impact, more content, and yes, more money. I believed that contentment was a recipe for mediocracy and synonymous with settling. I feared that allowing myself to be content would quell my desire to accomplish more and that "good enough" would be all I would ever achieve.

Over the past few years, I've begun to question that assumption. Can you be grateful and still want more? Are those things mutually exclusive? Can you be content without losing your ambition? Can you love your body and still want to lose weight? Can you love your job but still want a promotion? Can you love your partner and still want to improve your relationship?

The answer is yes. The key is to look at things just how they are with appreciation. Take my home. We moved into this house six years ago and did a complete renovation—the kind you see on TV. We took down walls with sledgehammers, tore out bathrooms, and added an entire second floor and a pool. It's been six years and we really haven't stopped. We drive our son crazy with our constant desire to improve, change, paint, build, and create. "You guys are never satisfied," he says. And he's right. *Let's add a garden or an outdoor shower. Let's rebuild the front walkway. I think we should re-stain the stairs, buy new outdoor furniture, put on a new roof.*

I love my house. I love the wall of trees that line our property and make my bedroom feel like a treehouse. I love the open, modern, uncluttered feeling of my living room. I love the soothing grey palate of the kitchen. I love the view from my bedroom window. I am grateful for my home every day and lying in the backyard fills me with contentment.

And yet. The driveway needs to be redone, I really want that outdoor shower, and don't get me started on the disaster that is the garage.

How are both of these things possible? How do we balance contentment and gratitude for what we have right *now* while still maintaining our ambition and desire for things to get better *then*?

The answer is in the heart of that sentence. We need to be better at being present in the moment and appreciating our now. And we need to keep our eye on the horizon and keep chasing big dreams.

Yup, I have learned that I can be grateful for my home, content in its embrace, and still want to do more. I have learned that gratitude, contentment, and ambition are not mutually exclusive.

On today's walk, think about your feelings about whether or not you can be content and ambitious.

Walk # 89: Be All In

I start new projects with a lot of enthusiasm. I am always the person in the room jumping up and down with excitement at the chance to learn something new or tackle a new project. More often than not, they are my ideas.

Let's renovate the bathroom.

Let's learn to ski.

Let's plan a picnic, write a book, or put on a show.

Let's start a company.

Over the years, I've learned to tamp down my enthusiasm and my excitement. Why? Two reasons really. First, I've been burned before. I've started so, so many projects that haven't worked out as planned.

There was the bathroom in our old house. "Let's paint it grey," I said. "It will be beautiful and calming." So off Eric and I went to the paint store to select a rich, dark grey. I swear, it looked great in my head but once on the walls? Dark, dreary, and awful. It took four coats of white to paint over it. But I had been so excited. It had been so beautiful in my mind.

When I was in law school, I started a business with my sister and now ex-husband making screen-printed t-shirts. The printer ripped us off, stole our designs, and never delivered the shirts. But I had been so excited. It had been so successful in my mind. And that first marriage? Who doesn't go into a marriage believing in your "happily ever after"?

And so, I've been burned before. I've started a dozen businesses that haven't worked. I've written a hundred articles that were terrible. I've begun writing several books that never got completed. I've hosted parties that were flops, taken trips that have been disasters, and cooked dinners that were inedible. I've made parenting mistakes, relationship mistakes, business mistakes. And don't even get me started about the "diets" that have failed.

All of this truly can tamp down your enthusiasm. Because when I think of something new, when I take on a new project, now there is that little voice in my head that says *well, sister, it hasn't worked before, so what in the world makes you think it will work this time?*

I always want to share my enthusiasm and bring others along for the ride. With pretty much the single exception of this book, most of my projects involve a "let's" or a "we" or an "us." And sometimes those projects don't work out. And people think "Oh, there she goes again." It's embarrassing to fail, and frankly, the more enthusiastic you are about a project and the more you share that enthusiasm, the more embarrassing it can be.

So you learn to tamp down your enthusiasm. To quiet your voice. To put a lid on your excitement. You have the little voice in your head saying "Just think about all of the things that haven't worked before and remember, this one might fail too" and the other voice that says "It will be so embarrassing to tell everyone you are doing this and then for them to see you fail."

Recently I attended the funeral of a spectacular man. He was the father of a dear family friend who impacted all of those he touched and among the many lessons to be learned from his life, one stood out for me.

As the pastor closed the service, she told one final story. At 85, Ed had been diagnosed with a serious heart problem and he had two choices: he could opt for medication which would likely extend his life but compromise its quality or elect to have a risky surgery that, if successful, would give him a quality of life for years. After weighing the options, he opted for the surgery. The pastor went to visit him the day before the surgery. They talked and laughed and prayed together. And they also talked about Ed's decision to go forward with the surgery. "I'm all in," he said. And that was how he led his life—all in. When he took on a challenge, made a decision or saw someone who needed help, he was "all in."

Those voices in your head that tell you that you can't do something? Ignore them. The fear that bringing your full self to a project, taking the biggest swing you can, sharing your enthusiasm with all who will listen, and then failing will be embarrassing? Ignore it. Be all in.

On today's walk, consider whether or not you tend to tamp down your enthusiasm for new adventures, challenges, and projects.

● ● ●

Walk # 90: Be 15 Minutes Early

Oh, the poor white rabbit. Always late. No time to say hello, he scurries in a constant state of stress.

I'm late, I'm late for

A very important date.

No time to say hello, good-bye,

I'm late, I'm late, I'm late,

I'm late.

Recently Eric and I traveled to a funeral. The trip required three ferries: the first two are short ferries that run continuously, no reservation needed. The third ferry runs hourly and requires a pre-paid reservation. If we missed that ferry, we'd miss the funeral.

For the first two short ferries, you typically pull up to the dock, wait under five minutes for one of the two constantly-moving ferries, drive aboard, and are on your way. But not that day. That day, only one ferry was operating, which slowed things down by half. And then there was a cement mixer that took forever to maneuver onto the tiny ferry.

Eric was beside himself, worried that we would miss our reservation for the big ferry and miss the funeral. But we didn't. We made it with barely any time to spare, but we made it. Because we had left earlier than necessary and built in some time for the unexpected.

I hate being late. If I have a 10:00 AM meeting, I will arrive at 9:45 AM to scope out the area and be sure I know exactly where I'm going. If I have a 3:00 PM doctor's appointment, I will arrive at 2:45 PM because I know there's going to be paperwork. On our first date, Eric found me seated at the bar of the restaurant where we were to meet, sipping champagne, and reading a book. He swears that was the moment he decided I was the girl for him.

Being fifteen minutes early does so many good things. Being early reduces your stress and minimizes that cortisol dump—the stress hormone—you feel when you are late for something. Unlike the poor white rabbit, being early gives you the chance to take a moment to talk to people. The chance to say more than "hello" and "goodbye." The chance to connect.

Being early lets you take control of a situation. When I was practicing law, I would always be the first to arrive for a meeting. I would go into the conference room, choose the seat I wanted, and set my documents on the table. When other people walked in, I was already there, poised and ready.

Scheduling to be fifteen minutes early means that when things don't go exactly as planned—when GPS sends you astray, when your kid needs a potty stop, when a cement mixer has trouble getting off the ferry—you will still be on time.

Be fifteen minutes early. I know that for some people, being on time—much less fifteen minutes early—is a challenge. Perhaps you get so caught up in what you are doing that you lose track of time. Maybe you have difficulty accurately estimating how long a task will take or how long it will take you to get someplace. Maybe you have three-year-old twins, in which case getting anywhere is a challenge and getting someplace on time almost impossible.

Or maybe you just don't think it's important. But it is. Being late causes you unnecessary stress and it inconveniences other people, both of which can be avoided with better planning and better tools.

Here are three tools to try:

- There are apps that enable you to put in the time you would like to arrive at a destination and will then calculate what time you should leave and, if you wish, put an alarm on that will tell you when it is time to go.

- Instead of putting the time something starts on your calendar, put the time you need to leave or begin to prepare.

- Practice showing up a little bit early and begin to build in that habit of being on time or, better yet, early. You'll likely come to appreciate the reduced stress you experience and be encouraged to continue to build a new timeliness habit.

I know what you are thinking. Other people are late all the time, so if you are prompt or even early, you might be the one waiting. But that's okay, truly. When I meet friends to walk, I am almost always there first. Some days, I take that five minutes to check my email. But other days, I take those few minutes to take a few deep breathes and reach my arms to the sky to greet the day.

On today's walk, think about how being late has added stress to your life and, if you are someone who is chronically late, spend a bit of time thinking about why.

Walk # 91: Celebrate the Small Wins

Yesterday, I solved a major hurdle in bringing our new business to life. It has been months of struggle. I've had dozens of calls, spent hours researching, asked hundreds of questions and have gotten hundreds of different answers. Yesterday, I found a solution.

I should have felt fantastic. I should have taken the afternoon off or, at the very least, taken a long walk in one of my favorite places. But I didn't. Instead, I checked it off my list and asked myself "what's next?"

Most of us launch from one task to the next, barely stopping to acknowledge the big value of the little wins along the way. This failure to celebrate our small successes is self-defeating.

In 2007, researchers Teresa Amabile and Steven J. Kramer conducted a study in which they analyzed nearly 12,000 diary entries made by 238 workers to uncover what it is that inspires people to be more creative and productive at work. As reported in the Harvard Business Review, the results were surprising. The most important motivator wasn't the pressure to perform or fear of failure. It wasn't a great work environment, incentives, recognition, benefits, or management support. Instead, what proved to be the single most important factor fueling motivation and momentum was whether or not people felt like they were "making progress in meaningful work." The more frequently people experienced that sense of progress, the better they performed in the long run. They dubbed it the "progress principle." The lesson is clear: in order to stay motivated, we need to recognize and celebrate momentum. The small steps. The little wins.

We don't do this enough. Too often, we are so focused on our larger goals that the small milestones feel inconsequential and not worthy of celebration. But they are. If our goals are big, the journey to achieving them will be long. If we focus only on what is left to do without savoring what we have accomplished, we rob ourselves of much of the fun along the way, and our most powerful motivator.

So why don't we? First, we are all so busy, and as soon as we've finished meeting one challenge, we are onto the next. Who has time to stop and celebrate?

Second, we think celebrating tiny wins is silly. If my goal is to write a book (this book, in fact) and I have tens of thousands of words to go, isn't it silly to jump up and down and celebrate a measly 1,000?

Third, we are afraid that stopping to celebrate the little wins will make us take our foot off the gas. If you want to run a marathon, will celebrating one mile make us feel like that is good enough?

Nope. The evidence shows that celebrating the small steps creates a success loop where one success leads to another and another. And besides, celebrating is fun. It feels good. And we deserve every good feeling and every moment of joy that we can grab.

On today's walk, think about all of the small wins you can celebrate. Rejoice in the one-mile walk you took even when you didn't feel like it. Celebrate getting through a full day without a chocolate chip cookie, yelling at your kids, or spending more than 30 minutes scrolling social media. Resist the urge to think "it's only one day," "I have so much more to do," or "what's next," and take a moment to relish your accomplishments. And when you return from today's walk, give yourself a gold star for a job well done.

Walk # 92: Wake Up and See Something Different

By now, you are probably pretty familiar with my morning routine but bear with me. Most of my days go like this: Wake up at 5:00 AM. Flip the coffee pot to "on." Let the dog out. Empty the dishwasher. Sit for a 10-minute meditation. Sit at my kitchen table and make an entry in my gratitude journal. Read five pages of whatever book I am reading and take notes. Write a minimum of 600 words. Text my dad. Make my daughter's lunch for school. Blend up a morning smoothie. Wake the kids and see them off to school. Work until 8:30 AM. Head to the gym. Go to the office. Eat a protein bar. Answer emails. Meet with my team. Eat lunch. Hop on the afternoon's calls. Answer more emails. Go home at 3:30 to see the kids off the bus. Head out for an afternoon walk. Make dinner. Help kids with their homework. Answer more emails. Eat dinner. Clean the kitchen. Walk the dog. Set up coffee for the next morning. Shower and go to bed.

Wake up. Repeat.

There have been times over the past several years that I've tried to commit to posting something on social media every day. Social media experts have told me over and over that it is "good for my personal brand" and that consistency is key. And I've tried. Invariably, I start out strong but within a week or so I literally can't come up with anything interesting to post because most of my days follow the same exact routine. And seriously, how many images of me sitting at my desk, doing a pull-up, or walking the same two-mile dirt road do people want to see?

I am a creature of habit. I love my routines. They ground me and enable me to be super productive. I love dinner with my family, and I love that two-mile walk from the golf course to the bay beach. And I love my bed.

Breaking from my routine gives me anxiety. What if my kids need me and I'm not here? What if my dad (he's 90) gets sick and needs me and I'm not here? What if I don't get 600 words written every day and this book never gets finished? What if I die in a fiery plane crash? (I think about fiery plane crashes a lot).

Yet, it is critical that some days we wake up and see something different. We go through so much of our lives on auto-pilot, moving from one familiar place or routine to another. We drive the same route to work, stop at the same coffee shop, and walk on the same trail. These habits free our minds to think about other things while we move efficiently through our days, barely noticing our surroundings. When we break those routines, we force ourselves to pay attention. Things become clearer, more vivid, and more memorable.

Breaking your routine can also make you luckier. As we discussed a few walks ago, a tremendous body of research has established that much of the luck enjoyed by "lucky" people comes as the result of those people expanding their horizons, making changes to their routine, lifting their eyes up, and embracing chance encounters.

You will find that most of the new people whose influence has the potential to enrich your life in new ways will be found when you step outside of your comfort zone and the comfort of your daily routines. Your world view and ability to create will be fostered by the influences you will encounter when you step beyond the walls of your routine.

On today's walk, take a good look at your routines. Consider which ones give you the sense of comfort, ease, and productivity that you love. Acknowledge them with gratitude. But then, make a plan to wake up and see something different. Commit to a vacation or an adventure. A road trip. A visit to family you haven't seen in a while. A trip to someplace you haven't explored or a walk on down a new trail. And then, even when your whirlwind tries to pull you back, fear makes you want to cancel, or your habits and routines make it almost impossible to make a change, force yourself to wake up and see something different.

● ● ●

Walk # 93: Play the Long Game: Kid Version

Long before my husband and I had kids, we adopted a puppy. He was perfect with soft black curls, a white chest, and four white paws. He was a Portuguese Water Dog and we named him Kibo after the highest peak on Mt. Kilimanjaro. He was a dog among dogs. He loved to play and wrestle with other dogs and he loved to be with us. He never needed a leash. We would take him to town, and he would sit patiently outside of a store waiting for us. He understood more than 200 words and was a trained therapy dog who regularly visited a center for developmentally disabled adults. Daily, strangers marveled at how well behaved he was.

Having now raised three dogs and two kids, I know that raising a dog is not the same thing as raising a child. But there is one thing I learned in my earliest days of puppy parenting that has stayed with me all these years: don't let your puppy do things you wouldn't want your grown dog to do. Yup, it's cute when your puppy gnaws on your sleeve or hops up into your lap. It's adorable when he grabs your sock and runs, begging you to chase him, or when he jumps up looking for attention when your mother enters the house. But these things are not cute when he is 60 pounds with adult-sized teeth and can outrun you clutching your favorite scarf in his mouth.

The same lesson applies to kids. As soon as your kids are able to take responsibility and contribute in their own ever-evolving ways, you need to let them. That is not always easy. There will be years when letting your child take responsibility for things will invariably mean those tasks take longer and don't get done as well as they would if you just did them yourself. Give up perfection and expediency in favor of giving your child responsibility and independence.

Little children are hardwired to want to help. It makes them feel good. Yet all too often, in our rush to get out the door or get dinner on the table, we finish the task for them. "Here, Kevin, let me," we say with a hint of annoyance as we tie his shoelace or clean up his toys or finish setting the table. When we take a task away from our child and finish it ourselves, we communicate so many things—and none of them are good. We are telling him that he's not doing it fast enough or well enough, reminding him that we can do it better, and teaching him that he doesn't have to figure it out for himself because we will step in and fix it. If we do this often enough, he will simply stop trying. Instead, when it is time to go, he will sit by the front door waiting for you to tie his shoelaces because he feels either that he can't do it, or he knows you would rather do it for him.

Now take the shoelace tying situation and amplify it to all of the things that you snatch from your child's hands and say, with even that little hint of tone that seems to be born into every mom along with her first child, "Here, let me."

The more responsibility you can give your child as early as reasonably possible, the better. This will take patience in the beginning and will require that you accept that you will not get out the door as quickly as you would have had you just done it all yourself, and things will not be done exactly the way you want them.

Making their own beds is a perfect example. Once your kids are out of cribs and into toddler beds, you have two choices: make their beds for them or let them make their own beds. For many months, it will be much easier to simply make that little toddler bed yourself. But for many years, it will be much easier if your child learns to do it herself. Learning to straighten the blanket, fluff the pillows (don't ask me why, but kids love to "fluff" pillows), and tuck in their teddy teaches so much. It teaches them to care for their things and to develop routines that will make their lives easier. It teaches them the pleasure of coming home to a tidy room and the feeling of ownership over their domain. Yup, it would be way, way easier to make their bed for them. But as soon as they can do it themselves, even if they can't do it well, let them.

Play the long game. On today's walk, think about a couple of moments during the day where you can let go, quiet the "Here let me" voice and let your child get it done on their own.

Walk # 94: Play the Long Game: Adult Version

On our last walk, we thought about why it is important to surrender our quest for perfection in favor of our long-term goals for our kids so they grow up to be independent, resilient, and confident. Today, let's think about what playing the long game can mean for you.

The media is replete with tales of overnight success. Justin Bieber puts a homespun video on YouTube and becomes a bazillionaire. A couple of students found the company Rovio, release Angry Birds, and become millionaires overnight. Lana Turner gets discovered at a drugstore counter.

But here's the thing: behind every overnight success story are a thousand small things. Hundreds and hundreds of tiny steps taken every day toward a goal. There are very, very few true overnight successes and millions of stories of success, which though they seemed to appear suddenly, are actually the result of years of genuine, quiet, and persistent hard work.

To have the life you want, to achieve the dreams you have, and to accomplish all you long to accomplish will require that you make tens of thousands of tiny choices that, while they might not align with what you want at that moment, align with your bigger goals.

This is not easy. We live in the moment and we want what we want. And oh, do most of us have a knack for making excuses along the way.

"I will skip my walk just this one day."

"It's Charlie's birthday, so I'll just have this one piece of cake."

"I will start working on my book when I can find a few hours to 'focus'."

"I will start working on my degree when my youngest goes to school."

"I will clean out the garage when I have time."

"I will start tomorrow."

But here's the thing. Dreams are built one brick at a time. That means that in order to achieve those dreams, you are going to have to make a hundred choices that align with your goal, even when those choices don't align with what you "feel" like doing at that moment. Every day you have to lay one brick down. Sometimes—okay, often—you are not going to feel like doing those things. You are not going to want to say no to the chocolate cake, take the walk in the rain, or study for the exam. Chances are, you'd rather eat the cake, relax on the couch, or watch the TV.

Build your dream house brick by brick.

On today's walk, think about a longer horizon for your dreams and commit to playing the long game. Then identify one single, specific change you can make in your daily routine that will be one metaphorical brick laid down in furtherance of your goal. And start doing it. Every day.

Walk # 95: Believe in Yourself and the Truth About Everyone Else

I suspect that there are some days you walk around thinking that everyone else has it together. Well, maybe not *everyone else*, but at least some people. Like the mom rocking mascara, lipstick, and a perfectly-styled high ponytail on the school drop-off line who makes you realize you haven't brushed your hair since the day before yesterday. You tell yourself all kinds of negative things about yourself as you make up all kinds of things about her.

Or perhaps, like me, you recently received an invitation to a reunion of a dozen women with whom you worked a decade ago, which prompted you to scroll their social media profiles to see their overwhelming success as you wonder how exactly you are going to make payroll of the company you founded. You create stories in your head of their perfect lives, satisfying jobs, huge bank accounts, perfect children, luxurious vacations, and beautiful homes. Your internal critic fires herself up and begins a recitation of all of the things you could have done or should have done. You review your failures, shortcomings, and bad decisions, ultimately concluding that you just aren't good enough. You begin to believe that because you *feel* unworthy you *are* unworthy.

But that's simply not the case. Everyone has those feelings. Everyone. And our feelings of insecurity and inadequacy are rarely based on fact.

Here's an example. Most of us would agree that the models who grace magazine covers are objectively beautiful. So, if insecurities were based in fact, models would not feel insecure about their looks, right? And yet, according to supermodel Cameron Russell, models "are the most physically insecure women on the planet."

Having feelings of inadequacy doesn't make you inadequate, it makes you human. It's what you do with those feelings that matter. You need to look them in the eye and call them out. I know, I know, easier said than done. Believing in yourself is, as most things, an act of will that, for most of us, requires constant practice and regular vigilance.

On today's walk, think about all of the things you like about yourself. Don't be shy, you don't have to share this with anyone. And if you are tempted to say, "I hate everything about myself," then put the pity party away and start coming up with things. Little things and big things. Do you have a fabulous laugh or pretty feet? Are you a good mom at least some of the time? Did you make your daughter a great school lunch this morning? Are you smart, creative, or kind?

You might find yourself tempted to add a "but." For instance, "I like my feet but I don't like my legs." Or "I like my house but wish it was bigger." Or "I'm a good mom but I hate it when I lose my temper." Fight the urge. No buts today.

Once you've thought about as many things that you like about yourself as possible, move on to consider things that you have accomplished that took work. Saved money and bought a house. Finished college. Painted a mural. Had a baby. Deadlifted 150 pounds. Raised a good person. Earned a promotion.

When you get back, capture those thoughts below. And then—and here is where the act of will comes in—when you are feeling down, when you are feeling like a failure, or like you are not enough, pull out this list and read it. And then tell yourself—literally tell yourself—that you are good enough. You may have to tell yourself these things several times a day. You might have to write a few of your accomplishments and awesome traits on your bathroom mirror. You might need to develop a morning meditation practice where you close your eyes, breathe deeply and repeat these things to yourself every single day.

● ● ●

Walk # 96: Be the Person You Want to Be, Not Necessarily the Person You Are

At about 11:00 this morning, I thought *"Wow, I'd love another cup of coffee,"* although I'd already enjoyed my usual two cups. I really do love coffee. But the person I want to be would drink a cup of detox tea (which I also love, just not as much as coffee) so I decided to be the person I want to be, rather than the person I am, and brewed a cup of licorice detox tea.

Yes, it's important to be true to yourself. To accept yourself. However, if there are things you'd like to change, shift, or improve, you can make huge strides simply by acting like the person you want to be.

If the person who you *are* is someone who grabs a donut on her way to work, but the person who you *want to be* fuels her body better, then tomorrow, be the person you want to be and grab a Greek yogurt instead of a donut. If the person you are sees the glass half-empty, but the person you want to be sees the glass half-full, then next time the opportunity presents itself, make a conscious decision to be the person you want to be and say something positive and optimistic. If the person you are is grouchy, but the person you want to be is cheerful, force your face muscles to smile and often your mood will follow.

Sometimes action follows mindset and we've talked a lot about mindset during our many walks together. But mindset can also follow action and sometimes, if you wait until you feel like eating a Greek yogurt instead of a donut, you might wait a long time. So instead, just start acting like the person you want to be.

It begins with developing clarity around the person you want to be. Who is she? What does she do? How does she spend her time?

On today's walk, think about the characteristics of the person you want to be. Don't think about accomplishments or goals, just think about the type of person you want to be. Here are a few of mine:

- I'd like to be a person who eats lots and lots of fruits and vegetables.
- I want to be a person who works with focus and efficiency.

- When I'm with my kids, I want to be one of those moms who is really "in the moment" with them.
- I want to be the most positive person I know.

When you get back from today's walk, write them down below and on an index card and put it right where you can see it. On your mirror, next to your computer, in your car.

Then, practice being the person you want to be, rather than the person you are. With practice, you will become her.

● ● ●

Walk # 97: Everyone has a Plan Until They Get Punched in the Face

While I loathe to quote fallen boxing superstar Mike Tyson, he is credited with once uttering words that have had a profound influence on my life: "Everyone has a plan until they get punched in the face."

Yup, you are going to make plans. You are going to set your goals and define your path. You are going to have a dream and a vision for your future, and you are going to go after it. Before you go to bed, you are going to write down the five most important things you plan to accomplish the next day in furtherance of your dream and your goal and you are going to wake up the next morning to the dreaded snow-day voicemail. Or a six-year-old with a fever. Or a broken water heater or flat tire. Or a suspicious mammogram.

You are going to be challenged.

You are going to be interrupted.

You are going to have setbacks.

You are going to try things that don't work.

You are going to hear a voice in your head that says, "This is too hard."

Someone is going to tell you your dream is silly, or your goal is impossible.

You are going to get frustrated.

You are going to be punched in the face.

You are going to be tempted to give up.

Here's how to reach your goals and chase your dreams despite all of this: Don't give up.

I'm sorry. I know you hoped I had some magic formula. Something that would make this all easy. But I don't. Big goals, big dreams are hard. They take work. Lots and lots of work. Want to lose 50 pounds? Lots of work. Want to lose 100 pounds? Even more work. Want to write a book? Lots of work. Want a new career? Lots of work. Want a beautiful house and a lovely garden? Yup, work. Want to launch a new company that improves the lives of millions of women? So. Much. Work.

But here's the thing: it's just work. It's just putting one foot in front of the other.

I remember a meeting I had with a very successful guy in the digital media space when we were just starting Macaroni Kid. He was thinking about investing in the company and, though he ultimately chose not to, he gave me a very good piece of advice.

"The companies that succeed," he said, "are the ones that stick around."

So, here is the ultimate secret to success: just don't give up. Don't quit. Don't stop trying new things. Don't stop exploring, testing, innovating, and taking risks.

But you can't try them in a half-assed way. You have to go from one to the next and give each effort everything you've got. As Winston Churchill reminds us, the path to success requires "stumbling from failure to failure with no loss of enthusiasm."

People will look at you like you're crazy. People will roll their eyes and say, "There she goes again." People who care about you will say "Are you sure you want to try another diet? Launch a new business? Take a new risk?" Some will ask because they want to protect you from the pain of failure. Some will ask because they are afraid of what your success will mean for them. Some will ask because they just don't get it. Ignore them and do not give up. It is the only way.

On today's walk, think about what not giving up looks like for you. Consider the stumbling blocks that are likely to get in your way and promise yourself that you will take your punches, deal with the challenges, accept the setbacks, embrace the failures, and never give up.

● ● ●

Walk # 98: Break out the Club

Jack London is crediting with saying "You can't wait for inspiration, you have to go after it with a club." We've talked about so much over the past 97 walks. We've talked about finding your dream, embracing your dream, managing obstacles, becoming happier and more productive, silencing the naysayers, and clearing the clutter. But in case you need a primer, a refresher, or a simple guideline to put on your bathroom mirror and look at every morning, here is how you achieve the life you want. Each step is pretty straightforward and pretty simple, though don't get me wrong, executing it is, well, not as easy.

First, know what you want. To know what you really want, you need to silence the naysayers and put aside guilt, shame, or any feeling that your dreams are too big. You need to connect with your truth and face—and overcome—your fear of failure. And, at some point, you must choose. You must say to yourself and to the universe, *this is what I want.*

Second, you must know why you want it. You have to dig deep and find your "why." And it can't be because someone else wants this, or because this is what you think you're supposed to want. This has to be your why and it has to be bigger than you. If you want a bigger house or more money for the sake of a bigger house and more money, you are going to have a really, really hard time doing the hard work needed to get there. If you want more money because you want your daughter to be the first in your family to graduate from college and pursue her dream to develop artificial intelligence software at MIT, well, that will get you out of bed in the morning.

Third, you must develop a clear path. You must break down that goal, that vision, into actionable pieces. You must identify all of the steps forward that you can take to get to that goal or to realize that vision. You must write those steps down and then you must keep revisiting that list, checking things off, and adding as you go, as new opportunities present themselves or new challenges and obstacles appear along the path. This is a constant, evolving, and deliberate process.

Fourth, you need to embrace a bias toward action. You cannot sit around your house wishing for things to be different. You can't lose hours of time on social media. You can't sleep in or watch three hours of television. You must take action. Consistent, purposeful, ongoing action. Even at the moments when you are not sure which step in the plan you should take next, take one. Move forward. Send the email. Register for the class. Apply for the speaking gig. Write the next page in the book. Clean the junk drawer. Turn down the ice cream cone and go for the walk. Take action.

Fifth, protect your energy. Goal crushing is hard work. That is why the vast majority of people give up on their dreams. But not you. You need a solid base of energy to do the work that it takes. Protect your energy by protecting your time. Protect your energy by fueling your body well. Protect your energy with exercise and nutrition. Surround yourself with people who build you up. Protect your energy by prioritizing rest, recovery, and sleep.

Finally, you simply can't give up. There is no secret sauce, magic bullet or easy solution. There is no simple path. When the going gets tough—and it will—you simply can't give up.

Ultimately, you will achieve your goals and change your life by sheer force of will. By determination. And here's the thing: if you don't want it badly enough, you will never do the work. And that's okay, that means that dream or that goal simply isn't important enough to you. Own that. You will never lose weight because society tells you that you should, you will lose weight because you realize, on the deepest personal level, that you want to ride a rollercoaster with your daughter or dance at your son's wedding. You will go back to school and get a law degree because you have a desire to right the injustice in our world. You will save money for your first Caribbean vacation because you know you can't go through this life without feeling the white sand beneath your feet and the ocean spread out in front of you. Not because you want to see those things—because who doesn't—but because you know that your life will not be complete until you do. You write a book because you have something inside of you that you absolutely, positively, must share.

On today's walk, ask yourself, once again, what do I want? What do I really, really want? What will get me out of bed at 5:00 AM, excited to rock the day?

Walk # 99: A No-Rules Day

During the past 98 walks, we've talked and thought about big, important things. Dreaming big, working hard, and being true to yourself. We've considered the importance of developing clarity, identifying what you want, and doing all of the hard work.

When we started on this journey, I told you that I expected there would be a few dozen of the 99 Walks in this book that truly resonated with you and enabled you to begin making real changes in your life. Assuming I was right—and I suspect I was, because you are still with me—then you are working really, really hard because, well, really hard work is what really big dreams take.

I've thought a lot about the idea I wanted to leave you with today, on our last walk together, and it is this: sometimes you have to have a no-rules day and prioritize fun and relaxation over productivity and purpose.

The idea of a "No-Rules Day" began one dreary February day when my kids were young. It was winter break, we were trapped at home and I was tired of being the screen, food, and shower police. So, when the kids got up, I announced that it was a "No-Rules Day." They looked at me, confused. "Does that mean I can have ice cream for breakfast?" my son asked.

"Yup," I replied. And so, the day began.

And I realized that I needed a No-Rules Day too. So, I didn't get out of my pajamas. I watched TV with my son and played with my daughter's massive collection of stuffed animals. I ate what I felt like when I felt like it. I skipped the gym and my walk. I never opened my computer or checked in on social media.

We read books in the hammock, ate when and what we wanted (which, to my surprise, included a pretty healthy dinner for all), and the kids skipped their evening showers. Of the thousands of days I've spent parenting my two kids, I remember every detail of our first No-Rules Day together.

No-Rules Days have now become a thing. Something we do a few times a year. They are days when I'm not pushing, not striving, not asking myself "What can I do today to chase my goals"—days when I skip the gym, don't live by my calendar and sometimes, don't even get out of my pajamas. They are days when I simply do whatever I feel like doing.

You need these days and I promise you, the harder you work, the sweeter your No-Rules Days will be. Not because you are exhausted—because the hard work of chasing your dreams is the kind of work that fuels your spirit. But it is work. Lots and lots of work. You might not feel like taking a day off. You might worry that if you take a day off, you will lose momentum. I get it, I really do. The more engaged you are in the work you are doing—whatever that work is—the harder it is to walk away, even for a day.

But you will reap incredible benefits from making No-Rules Days part of your practice. No-Rules Days will fire up your energy and creativity. Improve your sleep. Increase your productivity. And, No-Rules Days are great for absolutely no other reason than that they are fun. And I promise—eating ice cream for breakfast or watching too much TV once in a while is not going to do anyone any harm.

On today's walk, think about the last time you had a No-Rules Day where you really did what you wanted, when you wanted. If it has been a while—and I suspect that it has—put one on your calendar when you get back.

● ● ●

Acknowledgements

Where to even begin.

First and foremost, to my love, my partner, and my rock. Thank you, Eric, for a lifetime of support and encouragement and for the lessons you've taught me, many of which have found their way into this book. Thank you for never laughing at my crazy ideas and only occasionally answering when I ask, "How hard can it be?"

Mason and Maddie, you guys are the funniest, smartest, kindest and best kids a mom could ever dream of having the privilege to raise. I'm beyond blessed to be your mom and I don't have words for how awed, inspired, and proud I am of you both.

Mom and Dad, the words thank you are woefully insufficient. The countless lessons you have taught me have also found their way into this book, and I am everything I am today because of you two.

Lele, thank you for always sharing your creative brilliance and Susie, for always letting me know you are in my corner, even when you are not on my coast.

Mary, a huge thank you for reading the very first cut of this book and for everything you do every day to keep the wheels on. Jamie, Megan, and Jessica, thank you for being part of this mission to change the world and for the laughs, inspiration, and countless Zoom calls. And last, but not least, Laura, thank you for pushing me to be better and always being so generous with your spot-on judgment.

About the Author

Joyce Shulman is a serial entrepreneur, idea junkie, addicted skier, CrossFitter, and recovering attorney.

As the founder and CEO of Macaroni Kid, she built a multi-million dollar media company that delivers hyper-local, community-focused content geared for moms to more than 570 communities across the U.S. and Canada. Her decade of work with women revealed two of the most pervasive challenges they face: women are lonely and are confronting a health and wellness crisis.

Through extensive research and her own personal experiences, Joyce discovered that walking is magic for women, and recently founded 99 Walks, a company on a mission to get a million women walking.

Joyce lives in Sag Harbor, New York, with her husband, two teenagers, and one slightly unruly, but very sweet, dog named Moose.

● ● ●